D1030393

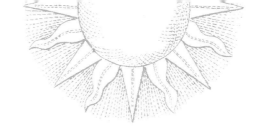

THE GREAT HISPANIC HERITAGE

Celia Cruz

THE GREAT HISPANIC HERITAGE

Isabel Allende

Simón Bolívar

Jorge Luis Borges

Miguel de Cervantes

Cesar Chavez

Roberto Clemente

Celia Cruz

Salvador Dalí

Oscar De La Hoya

Oscar de la Renta

America Ferrera

Francisco Goya

Ernesto "Che" Guevara

Dolores Huerta

Frida Kahlo, Second
   Edition

Jennifer Lopez

Gabriel García Márquez

José Martí

Pedro Martinez

Ellen Ochoa

Eva Perón

Pablo Picasso

Juan Ponce de León

Tito Puente

Manny Ramirez

Diego Rivera, Second
   Edition

Antonio López de Santa
   Anna

Carlos Santana

Sammy Sosa

Pancho Villa

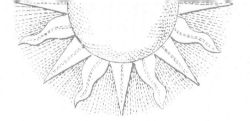

THE GREAT HISPANIC HERITAGE

Celia Cruz

Cherese Cartlidge

CHELSEA HOUSE PUBLISHERS

An imprint of Infobase Publishing

Celia Cruz
Copyright © 2010 by Infobase Publishing

Chelsea House
An imprint of Infobase Publishing
132 West 31st Street
New York NY 10001

Library of Congress Cataloging-in-Publication Data
Cartlidge, Cherese.
  Celia Cruz / Cherese Cartlidge.
    p. cm. — (Great Hispanic heritage)
  Includes bibliographical references and index.
  ISBN 978-1-60413-771-2 (hardcover)
  1. Cruz, Celia—Juvenile literature. 2. Singers—Latin America—Biography—Juvenile literature. I. Title. II. Series.
  ML3930.C96C37 2010
  782.42164'092—dc22
  [B]   2010007809

Chelsea House books are available at special discounts when purchased in bulk quantities for businesses, associations, institutions, or sales promotions. Please call our Special Sales Department in New York at (212) 967-8800 or (800) 322-8755.

You can find Chelsea House on the World Wide Web at http://www.chelseahouse.com.

Text design by Terry Mallon
Cover design by Terry Mallon/Alicia Post
Composition by EJB Publishing Services
Cover printed by Bang Printing, Brainerd, MN
Book printed and bound by Bang Printing, Brainerd, MN
Date printed: September 2010
Printed in the United States of America

10 9 8 7 6 5 4 3 2 1

Contents

Queen of Salsa

On the afternoon of July 22, 2003, a funeral procession made its way through the streets of New York City. Seven black carriages led the procession, followed by a white carriage pulled by two horses in plumed helmets. Twenty-two black limousines followed, while overhead four helicopters circled. The thunder and the large raindrops did not deter the 50,000 grieving fans who lined the streets, waving flags from countries all around the world. As an unusual way of saying farewell, some mourners threw handfuls of sugar into the white carriage as it passed. They all strained for a glimpse of the coffin, draped with a Cuban flag and carrying their beloved Celia Cruz.

New York City mayor Michael Bloomberg, New York State governor George Pataki, and Senator Hilary Rodham Clinton walked alongside the coffin. Bloomberg had ordered Fifth Avenue closed for the day—something usually only done for presidents, generals, war heroes, or astronauts returning

6

from the Moon. It was the first time that the avenue had ever been closed for a singer. After her death, Cruz's body had been taken on a tour of the United States so that fans could pay their last respects to her. Her public wake in Miami had brought 100,000 fans from around the world to visit the Freedom Tower, where her body lay in state. The tributes to her had lasted for a week, and the press dubbed her funeral "last tour of the Queen of Salsa."[1]

At St. Patrick's Cathedral in New York City, friends and family gathered for the ceremony presided over by Reverend Josú Iriondo, assistant bishop of New York. Inside the golden coffin lay a carefully dressed and made up Celia Cruz. She wore a white dress speckled with diamonds, a blond wig, and her favorite jewels; in her hands was a rosary with a silver crucifix. In the coffin with her were a picture of the patron saint of Cuba, Our Lady of Charity, and a copy of Cruz's final album, *Regalo del Alma*. Also in the coffin, in accordance with her final wishes, was a handful of Cuban soil.

Pedro Knight, Cruz's widower, walked arm in arm into the cathedral with Mayor Bloomberg. Dolores Ramos, Cruz's sister, was there and so was Cruz's manager, Omer Pardillo-Cid. Among the artists in attendance were Marc Anthony, Johnny Pacheco, Rubén Blades, Willie Colón, Antonio Banderas, Melanie Griffith, Patti LaBelle, La India, Ray Barretto, Jon Secada, Victor Manuelle, and Chita Rivera. So many people had come for the funeral that they could not all fit inside the church. Those who were outside listened respectfully through loudspeakers as Patti LaBelle sang "Ave Maria," while inside, the song brought Antonio Banderas to tears.

Who was this woman known as the Queen of Salsa, and why were so many thousands of people so deeply affected by her death?

BELOVED ARTIST

Throughout most of her life, Celia Cruz was immensely popular as a singer. She was also fiercely proud of her Hispanic

Celia Cruz is arguably the most famous female Latin singer in history. Known for her infectious smile, high energy, and outrageous wardrobe, she earned many nicknames during her 50-year career, including the Queen of Salsa.

heritage, and she helped instill that same pride in Hispanics the world over. She toured the globe and helped spread not only Cuban music—ranging from the rumba and guarachera to salsa—but also Latin culture. It was perhaps for this reason that fellow Cuban musician Paquito D'Rivera called Cruz quite simply "the most popular and most beloved Cuban artist of all time."[2] Cubans living abroad loved Celia Cruz because she reminded them of home. Hispanics living all over the world loved her because she reminded them to be proud of their heritage. Anyone who met her was instantly taken in by her broad smile, warm personality, and the genuine affection she felt for others, something that was apparent onstage as well as in person.

During a singing career that spanned more than 50 years, she earned a number of nicknames, each one reflective of her enormous appeal and her influence on the music scene. Throughout the years, she was known variously as *La Reina de la Salsa* (the Queen of Salsa), the Ebony Goddess, the Great Queen, the Tropical Goddess, the Queen of Latin Music, the Rumba Queen, and *La Gran Señora* (the Great Lady). Her favorite nickname, however, was *La Guarachera de Cuba*, because she felt it described her best. The guaracha is one of Cuba's most traditional musical styles, and throughout Cruz's career, she felt a connection to the music of her childhood.

"CELIA WAS CUBA"

Celia Cruz held a deep love for Cuba and was proud of her Hispanic heritage her entire life. Yet she left her beloved country in 1960, never to return. Things were different in the country after the revolution that installed Fidel Castro as dictator. Under Castro, musicians and other artists lost their artistic freedom and were required to perform songs supportive of the new regime if they wanted to find work. Requesting permission to travel outside of the country to perform became a nightmare of bureaucratic red tape and stifled the careers of many Cuban artists. For Cruz, living in exile from

CUBA'S GIFT TO THE WORLD

Celia Cruz once called music "Cuba's greatest gift to the world" and said that "music and dance are integral factors of the Cuban national character."* Music is very much a part of everyday life for Cuban people, who embrace their traditional styles of music that have spread their influence throughout the world. Among these traditional styles are the son, rumba, guaracha, danzón, and cha-cha-chá (these terms are also applied to the style of dance that went along with the music). The son is the most popular musical and dance form in Cuba. It developed around 1900, combining Spanish and African musical elements and featuring the tres, a six-stringed instrument similar to a guitar. In the 1920s, when Celia Cruz was a little girl, the son gained popularity in Cuba when it was played by *conjuntos*, which were sextets or septets. Cruz sang many songs in the son style with the Sonora Matancera orchestra in the 1950s and 1960s. A variant of the son, the rumba, also arose in Cuba and spread to the rest of the world as a ballroom dance in the 1930s.

Cuban music also includes the guaracha and the danzón. The guaracha, which arose in risqué Havana music halls in the 1920s and 1930s, features a fast dance rhythm and humorous, sometimes bawdy, lyrics sung by guaracheros. The danzón is another Cuban dance rhythm that became popular in the 1920s and 1930s; it spawned the danzonete craze made popular by famed singer Paulina Álvarez in 1929. The 1950s saw the rise in Cuba of the mambo and the cha-cha-chá, both of which sparked dance crazes that spread to the United States. All of these styles of music combined by the late 1960s to produce a new genre, known as salsa, of which Celia Cruz was acknowledged "the queen."

*Celia Cruz, with Ana Christina Reymundo, *Celia: My Life*. New York: HarperCollins, 2004, p. 26.

her beloved homeland was emotionally difficult. Although she became a U.S. citizen, she never forgot Cuba—the land, the music, and the people she left behind. She always carried these memories in her heart. One biographer noted: "Celia's well-known dream was to sing in a Cuba free of communism, and perhaps this could be the only disappointment she carried to her grave. To die far away from her country was very painful for this singer who so wholeheartedly loved the island that she hailed from."[3]

Omer Pardillo-Cid, whom Cruz considered an adopted son, acted as her personal manager and became the vice president of the Celia Cruz Foundation. He commented: "If you ever saw Celia Cruz somewhere in the world, you saw Cuba, because Celia was Cuba. Celia is the Cuba of yesteryear, the Cuba our parents dream of. . . . Her qualities as a singer are only superseded by her qualities as a human being."[4]

DESTINED FOR GREATNESS

It is a testament to Celia Cruz's enormous appeal as a performer that, despite the fact she never sang in English, she nonetheless became enormously popular in the United States. A *New York Times* reporter commented in 1998: "Many Americans have never heard of her, yet she has a nonstop schedule of sold-out concerts, a Grammy on a shelf in her New Jersey home and a street named after her in Miami."[5]

That Cruz possessed a great musical talent was obvious from a young age. Even as a young girl, growing up in a poor section of Havana, her clear, vibrant singing voice drew the attention of friends, family, neighbors, and strangers alike. One anecdote from her childhood serves as a good example of the kind of early attention young Celia commanded. On a shopping trip with her mother one day, Celia fell in love with a pair of white patent-leather shoes she saw through a window; unfortunately, her mother could not afford the shoes. As Celia would do countless times throughout her life, instead of

Miami is home to the majority of Cuban exiles in the United States, and many of its citizens were saddened when they heard the news of Cruz's death in 2003. Her remains lay in state in Miami's Freedom Tower for several days, during which an estimated 100,000 fans and admirers paid their respects to the singer.

giving in to adversity, she began to sing. An American tourist who heard her singing was so impressed by the emerging talent of this little girl that he bought her the shoes. These shoes not only represented the first time Celia earned something by singing, but they also sparked her lifelong interest in fashion.

Other people who heard her sing were equally impressed by her seductive voice. In 1950, she auditioned as the lead singer for one of the most popular orchestras in Cuba, the Sonora Matancera. Their leader, Rogelio Martínez, later recalled: "When that black woman opened her mouth, my hair stood on end. After I heard her, I featured her in my program at Radio Progreso in Havana, and I created a new repertory of songs for her."[6] In fact, when he told a producer from Secco Records named Sidney Siegel that he planned to record with Celia Cruz, Siegel asked if he was out of his mind. Siegel did not believe that a black woman could gain success as a singer, given the racism and sexism prevalent in Cuba at that time. Martínez, however, was so impressed by Cruz and so sure of her talent that he gave Siegel an ultimatum—produce the record or Martínez would find another record studio to do it. When Siegel listened to the demo tape of Celia Cruz singing "El Yerbero Moderno," a song that later became a huge hit for her all over the world, he called Martínez in the middle of the night and excitedly told him that he was going to give Cruz an exclusive contract.

A LIFETIME OF ACCOMPLISHMENTS

One reason so many people looked up to Celia Cruz was that she overcame a number of obstacles to become as successful as she was. She grew up in an impoverished neighborhood with a father who was adamantly opposed to the idea of her pursuing a career in singing. She had to help support her family while attending college and, later, the music conservatory. Perhaps most impressive, however, is that she went on to make a name for herself in a field that was at the time dominated by white men.

Part of her success was due to her ability to change with the times; she went from singing traditional Cuban songs early in her career to singing the new style of music known as salsa in the late 1960s and even recording with rock and hip-hop artists at the end of her career. She performed live in concert on five continents and was recognized the world over as a singer of extraordinary versatility.

Of course, the main reason for her phenomenal success was her powerful singing voice. When she sang, her raspy, piercing contralto filled venues big and small—from the tiniest nightclub in New York City to the largest arenas in Europe— and her audiences were immediately won over. Well-known bandleader Tito Puente, who performed with Cruz more than 500 times, recalled her unique singing voice: "I was listening to the radio in Cuba the first time I heard Celia's voice. I couldn't believe the voice. It was so powerful and energetic. I swore it was a man, I'd never heard a woman sing like that."[7] A concert reviewer for *Billboard* magazine once described her voice according to the following recipe: "Mix Ella Fitzgerald and Donna Summer in equal proportions, add a generous dose of Caribbean seasoning and then turn the heat way up and you have Celia Cruz."[8]

THE INCOMPARABLE CELIA CRUZ

Because Celia Cruz kept the year of her birth a closely guarded secret, people were left to guess at the age of this remarkable

AZÚCAR!

Beginning in the 1970s, Celia Cruz's spirited shout of "Azúcar!" at every concert became a trademark for her. *Azúcar* is the Spanish word for "sugar," one of Cuba's chief agricultural products. In an interview with *Billboard* magazine in 2000, Cruz explained the origins of her use of this word in her performances: "I was having dinner at a restaurant in Miami, and when the waiter offered me coffee, he asked me if I took it with or without sugar. I said, 'Chico, you're Cuban. How can you even ask that? With sugar!' And that evening during my show . . . I told the audience the story and they laughed. And one day, instead of telling the story, I simply walked down the stairs and shouted 'Azúcar!'"* From then on, audiences came to expect her to cry out this word, and they responded with laughter and applause when her full-throated shout would ring out.

*Quoted in Leila Cobo, "The Billboard Interview with Celia Cruz," *Billboard*, October 28, 2000, p. 50.

woman. She seemed ageless and tireless, performing hip-hop onstage a full 60 years after winning her first radio contest back in Havana. Singer Patti LaBelle once commented: "Celia Cruz was an amazing woman. She had the spirit and soul of a 30-year-old and she never stopped smiling."[9] The world-famous percussionist and bandleader Tito Puente was greatly impressed by her stamina onstage. In 1987 he told a *New York Times* reporter: "She keeps the musicians on their toes. We'll be huffing, exhausted, and she'll be on a roll, with more Tina Turner energy left in her than all of us together."[10] Her husband of 41 years, Pedro Knight, once commented on her extraordinary vitality:

There were times when she confessed to feeling sick before a performance. But when I expected her to be resting on a reclining chair or in her hotel bed, there she was on stage. Her strength was incredible. I won't forget a particular presentation in Spain when she had a fractured toe. It was impossible to cancel the show because we didn't know how the public would have reacted. But out of sheer spunk, she sang and danced as never before. One had to see her to believe it![11]

Celia Cruz was a legend in her own time. No one else can compare to her or even come close. She was adored the world over, with fans spanning the globe from Japan to Africa and from New York and Miami to Venezuela and Spain and everywhere in between. From her birth in a humble Havana neighborhood to her dazzling career that spanned seven decades to her spectacular funeral, she was a unique force on the music scene and in life.

2

Celia Cruz's Early Life

Celia Cruz always had a flair for the dramatic. She was a true entertainer with a knack for holding an audience spellbound, for being vivacious and flirtatious, and for captivating people's attention. The details surrounding the birth of this musical icon are no less dramatic than those of her life and her death.

Celia was born on October 21; for decades, that was all her fans knew about her birthday, because the exact year was in dispute. Throughout her long career, she refused to reveal what year she was born, wanting to keep her age a secret. Some sources gave the year as 1924, some as 1925, and some even as late as 1929. It was not until after her death that the year of her birth was verified on a copy of her birth certificate as 1925.

She was born Úrsula Hilaria Celia Caridad Cruz Alfonso in a poor section of Havana, Cuba. Her parents were Catalina

16

Alfonso and Simón Cruz. It is customary in Cuba for a child to receive the surnames of both parents, so Celia was christened with both Cruz and Alfonso.

Celia's mother named her after Saint Cecilia. In Cuba, it was a tradition for people to name their children after the saint that corresponded with the date of the child's birth—but Saint Cecilia's Day is November 22, and Celia was born a full month before that day. When a neighbor pointed out this fact to Celia's mother, her mother said it did not matter. She wanted to name her daughter after Saint Cecilia—the patron saint of music.

Catalina Alfonso was called "Ollita" by everyone who knew her. The nickname came from an orphan Celia's mother had adopted who could not pronounce "Catalina." Ollita had a beautiful singing voice, and she frequently sang to young Celia—even before Celia's birth. Celia believed she was able to recognize her mother's voice immediately, and she said that even as an adult, the memory of the sound of her mother singing soothed her.

TÍA ANA

Celia was very close to her mother's sister, Anacleta Alfonso, whom Celia called Tía Ana (*tía* means "aunt" in Spanish). The close relationship Celia enjoyed with her aunt had its beginnings before Celia was born. Tía Ana had a baby girl who died while Ollita was pregnant with Celia. Ana was heartbroken, and Ollita went to Ana's house to console her. Ollita explained to Ana her belief that when a baby dies, its soul returns. She told Ana to mark the baby in some way, so that she would recognize her when she was reborn.

At the baby's funeral, Ana did something that shocked everyone in attendance. Leaning over the casket and speaking softly to her dead daughter, she took hold of the baby's pinkie fingers and broke both of them. Ollita would later claim that the instant Ana broke the child's fingers, she felt her own unborn daughter jump inside her womb.

A few months later, on a very hot day toward the end of October, Ollita gave birth to Celia. Then one day, when Celia was a few weeks old, Ollita noticed something odd about the baby's hands. The pinkie fingers appeared to be twisted inward. Taking this as a sign, Ollita excitedly called Ana to tell her that her baby had returned.

Ana never had another baby. She became Celia's godmother, and Celia recalled in later years that she had two mothers when she was growing up—Ollita and Tía Ana.

THE CRUZ ALFONSO FAMILY

Celia was the second of four children and the only daughter of Simón Cruz. When Celia was born, her mother already had a daughter, Dolores Ramos, from a previous relationship. After Celia, Ollita gave birth to a son and a daughter who both died in infancy. There were two more children, a son named Bárbaro and a daughter named Gladys. Simón Cruz was not the father of Bárbaro and Gladys, nor of Dolores. Yet he and Ollita stayed married for the remainder of their lives, and together they raised all of Ollita's children.

In contrast to Celia's doting mother, her father was not a particularly warm or affectionate man. As a child, Celia was very close to her mother but felt a coldness and distance from her father. Yet she had no doubt that he loved her, and she held a deep love and respect for her father her entire life. He was a good man who worked hard to provide for his and Ollita's children.

Simón was a railroad worker. As a stoker for the Cuban railroad, he worked hard in a physically demanding job that did not pay much money. This led to a great deal of stress for him, because there were so many people living in his house, and Ollita was so busy taking care of everyone that she was not able to earn any money to help out.

Times were hard when Celia was growing up because Cuba's economy was not strong then. Cuba had once been a very wealthy country, thanks to the rich soil that had allowed

Cruz was born into a Cuba whose once-thriving economy had fallen into decline. As the Great Depression began affecting people worldwide, demand for Cuba's two most popular exports, tobacco and sugarcane, decreased and tourists no longer visited the island. *Above*, plantation workers harvest sugar cane from the fields in the early twentieth century.

crops to flourish for centuries. But with the stock market crash of 1929, the economy in Cuba began to change. Because of the Great Depression of the 1930s, the demand for Cuba's agricultural products, such as sugar and tobacco, declined. During World War II (1939–1945), Cuba's export of agricultural products declined further because of German submarine patrols in Caribbean waters. The war also meant a decline in tourism, another main source of revenue for the island nation. These circumstances led to increased unemployment throughout Cuba and hardships at home for many people, including the extended Cruz Alfonso household.

THE HOUSE ON SERRANO STREET

Celia grew up in the same house in which she was born, a modest house at 47 Serrano Street with a majestic kapok tree in the backyard. The door to the small living room faced the front sidewalk. There were also a dining room, two bedrooms, and one bathroom. It was not a very big house, considering the number of people who called it home. In addition to Celia and her siblings, many people lived in the little house: her mother and father, the orphan Ollita had adopted, and Ollita's mother, Dolores. In addition, various other relatives and their families would live there from time to time. These relatives included Ollita's sister and her four children and Celia's cousin and his two children. At times, up to 14 relatives in addition to the immediate family lived in the little house.

The windows of the house had bars on them for protection. A back corridor linked all the houses in the tenement building. Although it was crowded, and there was undoubtedly stress due to the economic difficulties, the atmosphere of the home appears to have been warm and loving. Celia once recalled, "There was a lot of love in that modest home."[12] Her mother's beautiful soprano voice filled the air, as did the aroma of her cooking. Although times were hard, the family ate plenty of rice and black beans, as well as papaya and fried ripe plantains. On special occasions, her mother would make a typical Cuban dish that would forever make Celia think of home: *ropa vieja*, which literally means "old clothes." This is shredded beef that is very juicy and tasty, and Celia would remember it fondly for the rest of her life.

SANTOS SUÁREZ

The Havana neighborhood where Celia was born and raised was called Santos Suárez. It was a poor, working-class neighborhood. People of many different races and ethnicities lived there. Celia and her family were Afro Cuban—descendants of Africans who came to the Caribbean either as slaves or as free immigrants.

The Santos Suárez neighborhood was always filled with music and was home to many musicians. Most Havana neighborhoods had their own *comparasas*, amateur groups that performed during carnival. This is an outdoor festival that has its roots in slave days: On Catholic holy days, slaves were allowed to dance to their own music in the streets of Cuba. Santos Suárez, too, had its own carnival parade group, called *Las Jornaleras*. During carnival season each year, the group would parade in conga lines through the streets with their loud drums and lively dancers in elaborate and colorful costumes.

Ollita did not allow her children to attend these parades because she worried the streets were not safe during carnival. People would get drunk, and sometimes violence would break out. Ollita also worried that if her children started dancing along behind the *comparasas*, they would lose track of time and of where the *comparasas* were going and would eventually get lost. But Celia adored the carnival in Havana, and she sometimes sneaked out with her sisters and cousins to see the parades. Not even her fear of being caught dancing with the *comparasas* could keep her away from the joyous festivities. The sights, sounds, excitement, dancing, and rhythms of the carnival stayed with Celia and had a lasting influence on her musical career.

In her autobiography, Celia recalled the excitement of the night when her Tía Ana sneaked her out of the house to attend the carnival:

> We arrived at the grandstand in front of the Capitol building, and the place was total madness, with everyone screaming, laughing, and dancing. It was wonderful. Still, there were a few drunken men who frightened me, so I grabbed my *tía's* [Ana's] hand and didn't let go. All the same, we danced and sang with the *comparasas* as we followed closely behind them. We didn't stop until our feet gave out on us. I don't remember what time we got home, but it was definitely past my bedtime.[13]

EARLY MUSICAL INFLUENCES

The *comparasas* who danced their way through the streets of Havana were not the only early musical influence in Celia's life. Music is an important part of life for many Cubans. Ollita's voice was not the only one to fill the little house on Serrano Street. Celia's father loved to sit on the patio after a long day of work at the railroad, smoking Havana cigars and singing traditional Cuban songs.

Celia herself hummed constantly, even as an infant. She would hum the lullabies she heard her grandmother, mother, and aunt sing to her. Celia hummed even before she could speak. Her grandmother Dolores told Ollita this was a sign that Celia would become an entertainer. Ollita encouraged Celia to sing whenever they had visitors to the house.

SANTERÍA

During the 300 years that slavery flourished before it was abolished in Cuba in 1886, approximately one million slaves were imported from Africa to Cuba, bringing their culture with them. Unlike in the United States, where Africans from one region were divided up to prevent the possibility of them banding together in revolt, in Cuba, slaves from one ethnic group were kept together. This allowed them to retain their native traditions and culture. African influence on music, dance, art, literature, and religion remains strong in the Caribbean today, and Cuba is no exception. One place in particular in which the African influence on Cuban culture can be seen is the Santería religion. Similar to Haitian Voudou and rooted in the Yoruba culture of West Africa, Santería developed in Cuba when slaves began to associate their Yoruba deities, or *orishas*, with Catholic saints. In this way, *santeras*, as followers of the religion are called, could continue to worship the *orishas* from their ancestral lands. In addition to the many *orishas*, Santería recognizes one supreme being, called *Olodumare*. The religion

Growing up, Celia would also sing her younger cousins and siblings to sleep each night. The children enjoyed her singing so much, however, that they would stay awake to listen. Celia had a strong voice, and it carried outside. People passing by on the sidewalk would stop to listen to her sing. They asked her father to leave the door open so they could hear her better. Celia was annoyed by this attention because she did not understand why the neighbors were out there—she did not realize it was her singing that made them stop. She was a little shy as a child, and she thought the neighbors were just being nosy.

One early musical influence on Celia came from a somewhat surprising source. In Cuba, street vendors, called *pregón* in Spanish, would call out to advertise their wares to shoppers passing by. These *pregón* likely sounded something like an

also includes elaborate ceremonies with feasts and sometimes ritual animal sacrifices.

So strong is the association of Santería with Cubans of African descent that many people assumed Celia Cruz was a santera. In fact, early in her career she recorded songs that were associated with the religion; yet she was not a follower of Santería. In her autobiography, Cruz writes: "I respect all belief systems and all religions, including Santería, but I am not a *santera*. I won't deny that I am somewhat versed in it. There is no such thing as a Cuban, regardless of his or her background, who doesn't know something about Santería."* Cruz recalled that as a child she was afraid of the *santeras*, and she would run and hide under the bed when she saw one. But she eventually began to identify with the music they played and saw it as a way of honoring her African heritage. The drumbeat and the songs honoring the Afro-Cuban saints filled her with inspiration when she sang.

*Celia Cruz, with Ana Christina Reymundo, *Celia: My Life*. New York: HarperCollins, 2004, pp. 25–26.

auctioneer or carnival barker, talking very quickly and in a rhythm that mimics singing. In fact, the cries of the *pregón* sounded like music to Celia's ears, and it is something she later incorporated in her own singing; she was well known for improvising rapid-fire lyrics while performing.

FIRST COMMUNION

Like many other Cubans, Celia's family was Catholic. As a child, Celia was eager to learn to read because she wanted to learn the Catholic catechism. She celebrated her First Communion in 1932 at Our Lady of the Miraculous Medal Church in Santos Suárez. This was a very special day for her; dressed in a flowing white gown with a veil, she felt like a princess. In her autobiography, Cruz says of her first communion: "I felt very calm and pure when the priest gave me the host. . . . I asked God for many favors during my lifetime, and from that moment on I have never strayed from my spiritual path and relationship with God, although I have always made it a point not to judge what others may or may not believe."14

GOING TO SCHOOL

Celia started public school when she was about six or seven years old. The school she attended, Santos Suárez's Public School No. 6, was called República Mexicana. Shy as a child— and also a little nearsighted—Celia at first was reluctant to leave her mother's side and go to school. However, she soon came to like school and enjoyed learning. After completing grammar school, Celia attended a Catholic school for girls called the Oblate Sisters. There she studied typing, shorthand, and English.

Celia did not have many friends as a schoolgirl and spent most of her time with her cousins, many of whom lived in the same house with her. She and her cousins enjoyed going to the movies, especially to see *The Lone Ranger* and movies starring Shirley Temple. Celia preferred watching comedies and musicals over the many war films that were popular at the time. As teenagers, she and her cousins also attended dances

HAVANA with PRICE TOURS

SO NEAR AND YET SO FOREIGN
90 Miles from Key West

VISIT CUBA

COURTESY CUBAN TOURIST COMMISSION

The unique cultural landscape of the Caribbean includes indigenous, African, and European influences. The music and dancing of island countries like Cuba are often a mix of folklore and popular trends. Cruz became a singer of several genres, including salsa and traditional Cuban music. *Above*, a 1930s Cuba Travel tourism poster features a caricature of a cuban entertainer.

at a neighborhood social club. They spent a lot of time singing the songs that were popular in Cuba during the 1930s and 1940s, particularly songs by Carlos Gardel, Paulina Álvarez, and Pablo Quevedo.

QUEEN OF THE CONGA

By the time Celia was a teenager, she had been singing at school concerts and neighborhood gatherings in Santos Suárez for several years. Her first official public appearance as a singer came when she was around 13 years old. Her older cousin Serafín, who lived in the little house on Serrano Street with Celia's family, encouraged her to sing in a radio talent show in Havana. The show, called *Los Reyes de la Conga*, or the Kings of the Conga, was held at Radio Lavín. Celia won the contest by a unanimous vote, and the judges named her the Queen of the Conga.

Although it was Celia's dream to become a singer, her father was against it. He wanted her to become a teacher. Because she wanted to make her father proud of her, Celia enrolled in teachers college in Havana, the Escuela Normal para Maestros. There she studied to become a literature teacher. But for Celia Cruz, the dream of becoming a singer never went away.

3

Pursuing Her Dream

When Celia Cruz entered teachers college, she was unaware of the real reason her father did not want her to become a singer. For reasons Celia did not understand until she was a little older, Simón Cruz did not view singing as a respectable career for a woman. Simón Cruz was much older than his wife and was very traditional. He worked all day long at the railroad, shoveling coal into the furnace of a rail car. Some of his coworkers were rather rough men who liked to frequent bars and nightclubs, visiting the showgirls—or, as they were also known, *mujeres de la vida*, or prostitutes. It was because Simón Cruz did not want his young daughter to gain an unfavorable reputation—or worse still, follow in the ways of the other showgirls—that he was so adamantly opposed to her pursuing a career as a singer.

27

TEACHERS COLLEGE, RADIO CONTESTS, AND CAKES

With her dreams of becoming a professional singer seeming to fade into the background, Celia Cruz began teachers college in the mid-1940s. At the Escuela Normal para Maestros, she was a good student and made many close friends. Even in teachers college, though, she did not stop singing altogether. Singing was so much a part of her life—and of her family's life—that it would have been impossible for her to stifle her voice. She sang at home, at church, and at neighborhood festivities, and people were starting to take serious notice of her musical talents.

One of these people was her older cousin Serafín, who had encouraged her to enter the contest at Radio Lavín, where she had been named Queen of the Conga. Serafín was so impressed by her voice that he entered her in another radio contest, *La Hora del Té* (*Tea Time*), without her knowledge. At that time, amateur radio contests were becoming very popular in Cuba. Still shy even in college, Cruz was very nervous about the contest at Radio García Serra, because it was only the second time she had sung before a panel of judges. She also knew that people who won these competitions were awarded wonderful prizes.

She dressed all in white: white dress, white stockings, and white shoes. She took her claves, or percussion sticks, with her, which helped calm her because they reminded her of her musical idol, Paulina Álvarez. She sang a popular Argentine tango called "Nostalgia," accompanying herself with her claves. She won the contest, and the prize was a beautiful cake from a Havana bakery. For Celia Cruz and her family, struggling to get by, a cake was a real luxury. She recalled years later that the cake looked like it was made of lace, with its white frosting and colorful flowers. The following month, she won a silver chain necklace in the final round of the talent contest at the radio station. The necklace was her first piece of jewelry.

After winning the Tea Time contest, Cruz realized that her singing could bring good things to her and her family, and she entered as many talent contests as her schedule at college would allow. Often, the prize was another beautiful cake, but she won other items as well: cans of condensed milk, chocolate bars, bread, soap, boxes of crackers, and other necessities. Sometimes, she would even win cash prizes. Her winnings were a boon for her and her family, especially the money, which she used to help pay for her textbooks and other expenses at teachers college.

PAULINA ÁLVAREZ

When Celia Cruz was growing up, the radio was the most popular form of entertainment in Cuba, and she spent hours at her Tía Ana's house listening to programs that featured orchestras playing popular music. Some of Ana's and Celia's favorite musicians were Antonio Arcaño, Abelardo Barroso, Fernando Collazo, Pablo Quevedo, and Arsenio Rodríguez. These musicians would later influence Cruz's style as a singer—but none would influence her as much as the great Afro-Cuban singer Paulina Álvarez.

Álvarez (1912–1965) was a soprano who was hired in 1929 by saxophonist Aniceto Díaz to sing the vocals on his song "Rompiendo la Rutina" ("Breaking the Routine"). This song was in the style of the instrumental danzón popular in Cuba at the time, but it broke with tradition by using a vocalist. The song became immensely popular and launched not only a "danzonete" craze but also the career of Álvarez, earning her the nickname "The Empress of the Danzonete."

Cruz was greatly influenced by Álvarez, who had broken ground by performing in public in Cuba in the 1920s at a time when women rarely did so. Álvarez used claves—two cylindrical pieces of wood that are struck together to produce a sound—and because Cruz admired her so much, she incorporated claves in her own performances. Cruz credits Álvarez as the singer she most tried to emulate, and she admits in her autobiography that she modeled her own performance after that of Álvarez.

Cruz's family was always happy for her when she would win a contest, and she felt like she was coming home to a celebration. Everyone would laugh and hug her in congratulation—everyone, that is, except for her father. While the other people in her family would get very excited when she won a singing contest, her father would remain quiet. She found his attitude hurtful, but she loved him and wanted to please him by becoming a teacher. All through college, as she won contest after contest, Celia Cruz fully expected that she would have to give up singing when she finished school and started teaching.

WORDS THAT CHANGED HER LIFE

One day in 1949, after she had graduated from teachers college, Cruz was asked to sing "República de México" at a public school graduation ceremony. After she sang the song, she approached a teacher she respected very much, Marta Rainieri, and asked her for advice on how to find a teaching position. The teacher's response to Cruz changed her life. Rainieri told Cruz that God had given her the gift of a beautiful singing voice and that she should not waste that gift by becoming a teacher. Then Rainieri said, "Sing, and in one day you'll make as much as I do in a month."[15]

Even though Cruz had never stopped singing while she was in teachers college, she had always thought she would have to give up her first love once she became a teacher. But the words that Rainieri spoke to her that day made her think about her life in a different way. That day, she decided once and for all to pursue a career as a singer; however, she saw her singing as a form of teaching, saying, "Through my music I can teach generations of people about my culture, and about how much happiness one can find by giving joy to other people."[16]

HAVANA'S MUSIC CONSERVATORY AND THE GOLDEN BUTTON

By the time Cruz graduated from teachers college in 1949, she was already attending the Conservatorio Nacional de Música,

Celia Cruz attended teachers college in Havana, Cuba. Despite the worldwide economic depression and the effects of the First World War, Havana was a bustling Caribbean city in the 1930s.

Havana's National Conservatory of Music. There she studied voice, music theory, and piano. She also took private piano lessons with a teacher her Tía Ana hired, but Cruz did not like the teacher and the lessons did not last very long. She was fortunate enough to begin studying piano then with a well-known composer named Óscar Muñoz Boufartique (he would later compose the song "Burundanga," which would become one of Celia Cruz's biggest hits). This, too, was a short-lived effort; when Boufartique told her she would have to trim her long fingernails if she wanted to learn to play the piano, Cruz refused to cut them. In later years, she revealed that one of her biggest regrets was that she did not learn to play the piano when she had the chance.

Cruz studied at the music conservatory until 1950. During this time, she began to perform publicly on a regular basis, and she gained valuable experience. Her older sister, Dolores, who also had great talent as a singer, was part of a neighborhood musical group called El Botón de Oro, or the Golden Button, and she convinced Celia to join the group. Each girl in the group wore a small, flower-shaped gold button—hence the group's name. The Golden Button sang at parties and other events in the Santos Suárez neighborhood. They were not paid for performing, but they did receive soft drinks, candy, and cake, and the girls enjoyed attending the parties. More importantly, however, was the invaluable experience Cruz gained performing in front of a live audience.

SINGING FOR RADIO

Cruz also gained experience by singing for radio. She had entered so many radio contests that she was already well known at several major radio stations in Cuba, among them Radio Cadena Suaritos, CMQ Radio Studio, Radio Progreso, and Radio García Serra. These radio stations began to hire her to sing for them. Sometimes she would work at a station for only a day, but often the job would last longer. She appeared regularly at CMQ, performing along with other artists on Sunday afternoons in a program called *Estrellas Nacientes* (Rising Stars).

Cruz learned many things about life as a performer at CMQ that would help her throughout her career. When she was not performing herself, she would spend hours observing the other performers, studying their techniques. In this way, she got a performance education at the radio station. Because everything on the radio was performed live, and

After leaving teachers college and enrolling at the National Conservatory of Music, Cruz began to concentrate on her training to become a singer. She had already performed several times on the radio, winning small prizes in singing contests, and she gained experience performing in nightclubs. *Above*, Cruz dances with nightclub patrons in Havana.

often in front of a studio audience, Cruz learned early in her career that things did not always go exactly as planned onstage and that performers had to learn to cover their mistakes. She also learned—the hard way—that a performer always had to be prepared. This lesson came one day at CMQ when Cruz's performance was considered subpar and she was gonged, a somewhat humorous sign that she should stop performing and leave. The pianist, who was overbooked that day, had refused to rehearse with her, and as a result she could not get her song, "Chiquilla," to sound right during the broadcast that night. Years later, she still recalled the humiliation of being gonged that night: "From that moment on, I would never record or perform anything if I hadn't gotten the tone right. It's amazing; that happened years ago, and I still haven't forgotten what I learned. I'll never, ever forget being gonged."[17]

MEETING HER IDOL

Celia Cruz used to go to the nightclubs and listen to music as a child, since it was legal for children to enter such establishments in Cuba. Later on, she would start singing at these same Havana nightclubs. It was at the world-famous Tropicana that she had the opportunity to meet and perform with her musical idol, Paulina Álvarez. The two of them appeared together along with another singer, Xiomara Alfaro, and the Riveros Orchestra. Cruz called performing with Álvarez a "wonderful experience" and said she finally got the chance to tell her how much she admired her; Álvarez, in turn, complimented Cruz on her voice, which meant a lot to Cruz.

ANACAONA

In 1949, Celia Cruz was part of an all-female orchestra called Anacaona. They toured the city of Maracaibo in Venezuela. The name of the group came from a legendary Cuban-Indian princess. It was founded by Conchita Castro in 1932, and all 10 of Castro's sisters were part of the orchestra at one time or another through the years. Cruz loved working with a large group of women, because it made her feel like she had 10 sisters of her own. Cruz only sang with Anacaona for a short time, but she would tour Venezuela again in 1949 with a different group.

LAS MULATAS DE FUEGO

Cruz soon joined another all-female group called Las Mulatas de Fuego, or the Blazing Mulatto Women. (The term *mulatto* refers to a person of mixed black and white ancestry.) While singing at the Tropicana, she had met the choreographer there, a man named Roderico Neira, who was known as Rodney. He had formed the all-female dance group and invited Cruz to sing with them in a show at the Teatro Fausto. They subsequently toured Mexico and Venezuela and were extremely popular in Latin America. While in Venezuela with Las Mulatas de Fuego in 1949, Cruz recorded several songs with the Sonora Caracas

SUN SUN BA BAÉ

Roderico Neira was a choreographer at Havana's world-famous nightclub, the Tropicana. He was known as Rodney, which was a combination of the first three letters of his first name and the first three of his last. In the late 1940s, he put together an Afro-Cuban musical revue called *Sun Sun Ba Baé*. An hour and a half long, the show featured modern dancers and Celia Cruz as the lead singer. Its roots were in Afro-Cuban religious rituals, and the composer, Rogelio Martínez, was rumored to have asked *santeros* to request permission from the traditional Afro-Cuban gods to perform the music onstage. The show became a sensation in Cuba. It opened with the famous Cuban dancer Olga Chaviano being carried onstage on a palanquin, or covered sedan chair, carried by one man at each of the four corners. Cruz would walk onstage, singing in Lucumí to the beat of drums while dancers wildly filled the stage.

The show opened at the Sans Souci nightclub, which was on the outskirts of Havana, but it soon moved to the Tropicana in Marianao, Havana's sister city. Owing to the enormous popularity of the show, Rodney was made director of choreography for the Tropicana.

Orchestra, the Leonard Melody Orchestra, and the singer Luis Alfonso Larraín.

THE SUPPORT OF HER FAMILY

Cruz says in her autobiography that she got her singing voice from her mother and her love of the stage from her Tía Ana. Celia had lived with her aunt for a while during her childhood. During this time, young Celia was always singing, but because she was shy as a child, she did not move around when she sang. Her Tía Ana told her to shake her body a little when she sang, rather than standing like a statue. From then on, Celia Cruz danced when onstage, gyrating and spinning in rhythm to the music.

Her mother and her aunt were firmly on her side. One family member, however, remained to be won over—Celia's father, Simón Cruz. For a while, he was ashamed of her career path and would not tell people his daughter was a singer. Then one day, he saw a newspaper article on Celia that talked about how talented she was. Because the article was so positive about her, he realized that she had not become a "lady of the night" and was still following a moral life. He confessed all of this to Celia that evening at home, and she finally understood the reason for his reservations about her career. And Simón Cruz, at last, realized that the only career his daughter was meant to follow was that of a singer. It was her destiny to be a singer.

4

The Sonora Matancera

Now that she finally had her father's blessing, Celia Cruz was able to pursue her dream of becoming a successful singer. By 1950, she had traveled all over Cuba to perform, as well as to Mexico and Venezuela, where she had recorded several songs. By the time she was 25 years old, she had already made a name for herself at radio stations and nightclubs all over Cuba, singing at Radio García Serra, CMQ, and Mil Diez (1010), as well as at the world-famous Tropicana nightclub. She was becoming a sought-after and well-known performer in Latin America and the Caribbean. It seemed that Cruz accomplished anything she set her mind to. Her dream of becoming a professional singer was now becoming a reality. Soon, she would set her sights on the world-famous Cuban orchestra, the Sonora Matancera.

RADIO CADENA SUARITOS

In 1950, Cruz was working at Radio Cadena Suaritos in Havana. The owner of the station, Laureano Suárez, was known simply as Suaritos. Cruz believed that Suaritos did not like her, because he only let her sing backup for the station's exclusive recording artists, including Amelita Prades and Candita Batista, and never allowed her to sing solo.

The first time Cruz heard the Sonora Matancera perform was while she was working at Radio Cadena Suaritos. Her cousin Nenita told her to tune in to Radio Progreso one morning if she wanted to listen to a really good orchestra. Cruz recalled years later that the moment she heard the Sonora Matancera play, she began to dream of performing with them. In fact, she had a dream in which she was singing onstage at Havana's Campoamor Theater in a flowing white gown, with the Sonora Matancera playing behind her. She interpreted this dream as a sign that someday she would actually sing with them. She became a huge fan of theirs and would go see them perform whenever she could.

It was around this time that the lead singer for the Sonora Matancera, Myrta Silva, left the band to go back to her home in Puerto Rico. Silva had been singing with the orchestra since 1947 and was quite successful with them, but she missed her native country and wished to return. She became a leading radio and television personality in San Juan and later provided voices for Hollywood cartoons. When Silva left Cuba, the Sonora Matancera began to look for a new lead singer. Celia Cruz knew that singing with the famous orchestra would give her career a huge boost.

AN AUDITION WITH THE SONORA MATANCERA

It would not be long before Cruz got the opportunity of her lifetime. In June 1950, a man came to visit her at work at Radio Cadena Suaritos. His name was Rafael Sotolongo, and he worked for the sponsor of the Sonora Matancera program at Radio Progreso. He made Cruz a proposal that she later recalled made her heart leap into her throat. He said the orchestra wanted her to audition as the replacement for Myrta Silva. Sotolongo told her to go to the Radio Progreso studio and ask for the leader of the Sonora Matancera, Rogelio

THE SONORA MATANCERA

The Sonora Matancera was founded in Cuba in 1924 by Valentín Cané, who played the timbales—snare drums, cowbells, and a wood block. Cané also played the tres, a guitar with three double strings. Through the years, members of the orchestra left and were replaced by other musicians. They played open-air concerts and also at dances, private parties, and festivals arranged by political parties. The Sonora Matancera began playing at CMQ Radio in 1950, but it was at Radio Progreso that they found their longest-lived gig: They performed and recorded there for 30 years. They also played at the Tropicana nightclub. They recorded more than 4,000 songs over the course of 60 years and were the most successful band from the Caribbean in history.

Although musicians "rotated" through the Sonora Matancera, there were several who made a lifelong career of the band. Pianist Lino Frías played with the orchestra from 1942 until 1977. Guitarist Rogelio Martínez joined in 1928 and later became the leader of the group, a position he held for 57 years. In 1944, the band took on a second trumpet player named Pedro Knight. That was the same year a massive hurricane devastated the island of Cuba. Many homes and businesses were destroyed by the terrible storm. Knight was playing trumpet for a traveling circus that was also destroyed by the hurricane. Because the circus could no longer pay him, Knight's life became very difficult. Often he had no money for food, and he ate only once a day—usually only a slice of bread and some water boiled with brown sugar. Knight was very fortunate indeed to have joined the Sonora Matancera. He stayed with the band until 1967.

Martínez—the same man who had composed the music for *Sun Sun Ba Baé*.

This was one of the biggest moments in Celia Cruz's young life, and she was understandably nervous. Because Sotolongo had approached her at work, she still had several songs left to perform that day at Radio Cadena Suaritos, but she was so nervous that she could barely sing. She decided to ask for advice on her audition from Rodney, the choreographer at the Tropicana whom Cruz knew from the *Sun Sun Ba Baé* show. She knew that Rodney and Martínez were good friends. Rodney agreed to help, and he introduced Cruz to Martínez the next day. Cruz was thrilled when Martínez gave her an appointment for an audition. It was like a dream come true for her.

Cruz dressed carefully for her audition with the Sonora Matancera, making sure to take a raincoat and umbrella to protect herself from the pouring rain. She arrived early for the audition, composed and dry. When she walked in to the Radio Progreso studio, the first person she saw was the handsome young trumpet player, Pedro Knight. She soon learned that he was always the first to arrive at rehearsals. Cruz recognized Knight from all the times she had gone to see the orchestra perform around Havana. She introduced herself and explained why she was there, and Knight asked to see her musical arrangements. Right away, Knight spotted a problem—all of Cruz's arrangements were for a 14-piece orchestra, and the Sonora Matancera had only 9 musicians. Despite the problem, Cruz sang several numbers with the orchestra that morning, then left and waited to hear back from them.

A ROCKY BEGINNING

For the next two weeks, while she waited to hear whether she had passed her audition, Cruz continued singing at Radio Cadena Suaritos. Then one day an article appeared in a newspaper that reported the Sonora Matancera had replaced Myrta Silva with a singer named Celia Cruz. When

When Cruz was given the opportunity to audition as the female singer of Sonora Matancera, one of the most famous Cuban orchestras at that time, she nervously sang for them. During that session, she met her future husband, Pedro Knight. *Above*, members of the Sonora Matancera in the 1970s.

Suaritos, the owner of the radio station, read the article, he immediately fired Cruz. This was extremely difficult for Cruz and her family, because the newspaper article had been a bit premature—her position with the Sonora Matancera was not yet official—and she had no other source of income. Her family depended on her financial help, and when Celia lost her job, it posed a real hardship for them.

Then at last, at the end of July, Cruz got word from Rogelio Martínez that the orchestra was extending an invitation to her to become its new lead singer. It is important to note that, like Myrta Silva, Celia Cruz was never an official member of the Sonora Matancera but rather a guest soloist performing with the orchestra.

Celia Cruz made her first public appearance with the Sonora Matancera at Radio Progreso on August 3, 1950. Her entire family came to see her perform, including both her parents and her cousin Serafín, who had helped her get started with her singing career. Sadly, shortly after Cruz's debut with the Sonora Matancera, Serafín died. He left five children behind. Cruz said of his death, "It is a pain that I always carry inside of me."[18]

A PUBLIC REACTION

People did not immediately accept Celia Cruz, a relative newcomer, as the replacement for Myrta Silva, who had been tremendously popular. Silva had a large following, and her sensual, almost erotic style of singing and moving onstage was very different from Cruz's. Celia Cruz had a rich, strong voice, and while she was known for being flirtatious onstage, her movements did not approach the suggestive ones of Silva. Another advantage Silva had was that she was white, which was a great advantage in Cuba at that time. Celia Cruz was black and also very slender—compared to the voluptuous Silva—and she did not fit the stereotypical ideals of beauty that were prevalent at the time. Many fans of Silva and the Sonora Matancera did not believe Cruz was the right choice for the new lead singer of the band. Some people even called or wrote letters to Radio Progreso to complain and ask for the return of their beloved Myrta Silva. They called Celia "skinny" and "ugly."

One former trumpet player for the orchestra, Calixto Leicea, recalled the reaction of an audience member one night after one of Cruz's early performances with the Sonora Matancera: "A man approached us to say, 'Hey, what a pity that Celia is so ugly.' Rogelio Martínez grabbed the man by the neck, and roughed him up for being so rude. How dare he? How is he going to say something like this about the orchestra's darling pet? She was not only talented, she was a beautiful woman, and she had always been beautiful."[19]

LA GUARACHERA DE CUBA

In the end, it was Celia's melodic voice that won people over. She had a powerful, piercing voice and was very charismatic onstage. Once they heard her sing, audiences loved her and became faithful fans.

At that time, it was popular to produce albums that contained different musical styles to appeal to a wider audience. Cruz recorded all these different styles with the Sonora Matancera—guaracha, danzón, son, cha-cha-chá, and rumba. By far her favorite styles were the rumba and guaracha. It was for this reason that Celia Cruz became known as *La Guarachera de Cuba*, which she later said was her favorite nickname of all.

The collaboration between Celia Cruz and the Sonora Matancera lasted 15 years. Celia recorded more than 180 songs with the band. Among the most successful of these were "El Yerberito" and "Burundanga." In 1957, she received her first Gold Record for the song "Burundanga," which had been composed by her former piano teacher, Óscar Muñoz Boufartique. She recorded 74 albums with the Sonora Matancera, releasing a new album every three months.

Celia Cruz's collaboration with the Sonora Matancera propelled her from a relatively unknown nightclub performer to a world-renowned singer. The collaboration also benefited the orchestra by bringing it into the limelight and elevating its popularity in Cuba and abroad. Through the years, the Sonora Matancera had more than 100 vocalists, but many people, fans and music critics alike, view the era that Celia sang with the Sonora Matancera as the orchestra's greatest years. During the 1950s, Celia Cruz continued to tour abroad, with and without the famous orchestra. She toured widely in South America, Mexico, and the United States, performing at New York's Teatro Puerto Rico, Caborrojeño, and Palladium Ballroom and at the Hollywood Palladium in California. She also recorded songs without the famous orchestra, including a 1952 collaboration with a well-known Haitian singer named

Marthe Jean-Claude, who had come to Havana at Cruz's invitation to sing at the Tropicana.

In her autobiography, Celia Cruz reminisced about her years with the orchestra: "The Sonora Matancera changed my life. Musically, the band was excellent. People still listened with awe to the music the Sonora recorded back then. I have always said that the Sonora was a great orchestra way before I joined it. I will always consider the members of the band my brothers."[20]

CELIA CRUZ ON-SCREEN

While she was singing with the Sonora Matancera during the 1950s, Cruz also began to sing in commercials. Again, her physical appearance would have an effect on her career. Although she was well known for her beautiful contralto singing voice, the producers of the commercials she sang for did not want to show her in the commercials. At that time in Cuba, many singers recorded jingles for cigarettes and other products, but the commercials shown on television never featured black singers. If the singer was black, the commercial would feature a white artist with a dubbed voice.

Cruz recorded jingles for companies promoting cheese, cigars, coffee, cologne, juice, rum, soap, and soft drinks; however, the companies producing the commercials did not want to feature Celia. It was a sign of how far she had come since her debut with the Sonora Matancera that the public would not accept Celia Cruz's distinct voice coming out of someone else's mouth. So the commercials instead featured dancers or models doing something else on-screen while Celia Cruz's voice played in the background. Cruz recalled years later, "It's amazing how things happen! In two years I went from being criticized by segments of the public because I wasn't Myrta Silva to doing jingles on television, which was then the most exciting medium around."[21]

In addition to recording jingles for television, in 1955 Celia Cruz appeared in a cameo role in her first movie. It was

When Cruz first sang with the Sonora Matancera, there was immediate backlash from the fans of the Cuban orchestra, who preferred the light-skinned, sensual Myrta Silva. It took several tries before Cruz won them over with her powerful singing voice. *Above*, a portrait of Cruz from her time singing with the Sonora Matancera.

a Cuban film called *Gallega en La Habana* (*A Spanish Woman in Havana*), starring Argentine actress Niní Marshall. More films followed, including *Affair in Havana*, starring John Cassavetes and Raymond Burr, in 1957. In these films, Cruz always appeared in the background as a singer onstage, often playing herself.

CHANGES IN CUBA

Now that Celia Cruz had become a successful singer, she wanted to do something to repay her parents for their support—particularly her mother, who had always encouraged her to pursue her dream. In the late 1950s, Cruz bought two plots of land in Lawton, a Havana neighborhood, and planned to build a house on one plot and plant a garden on the other. It proved to be a very frustrating experience for her because the contractors kept delaying the project, telling her they were having difficulties finding building materials. One day, Cruz performed at a party hosted by her friend María Hermida at a ranch outside of Havana. As it turned out, General Fulgencio Batista, the president of Cuba, was also at the party, and Cruz decided to ask him for help in getting the house built for her mother. After her performance, she met with Batista and explained her problem, and soon thereafter Cruz's contractors had all the materials they needed to complete the house. This house still stands today, and members of Cruz's family still live there.

Among the reasons the contractors had given Cruz for their difficulties in finding materials was that the political climate of Cuba was very unstable at that time. Batista had assumed power in Cuba in 1952, when he staged a military coup and became dictator. By the end of the 1950s, his corrupt government was facing the stirrings of another coup. Batista, Celia Cruz, and the rest of Cuba were about to undergo a revolution that would change Cuba forever.

5

Leaving Cuba

Life seemed to be going very well for Celia Cruz. She was riding high on a wave of popularity with the Sonora Matancera in Cuba and the rest of the Caribbean and Latin America. It so happened, however, that fate was about to deal her a heavy blow. Political events in Cuba were stirring that were about to create an upheaval in the country. These events would change the course of Cruz's career and have a profound effect on the rest of her life.

THE CUBAN REVOLUTION

The corrupt government of General Fulgencio Batista was becoming more and more unpopular with the Cuban people. One person in particular who was passionately opposed to Batista was a young political activist named Fidel Castro. He gathered an army of 82 men in Mexico, and in December 1956, this band of guerrilla fighters landed on the southern shore of

47

Cuba, where all but 14 were killed by government troops. The survivors fled to the mountains of eastern Cuba, where they continued their struggle to overthrow Batista.

There were several skirmishes between Castro's guerrilla fighters and Batista's troops over the next two years, and by December 1958, Castro was emerging victorious. As the guerrilla fighters took over one army garrison after another, and as Castro himself stood on the outskirts of Santiago preparing

FIDEL CASTRO

Fidel Castro was born on a sugar plantation on August 13, 1926, in the Oriente Province of Cuba. He was the third of seven children. His father was an immigrant from Spain, and his mother was a household servant. Fidel was an intelligent child but often got into trouble, so his father sent him off to a Catholic boarding school with strict discipline. Fidel Castro entered the University of Havana Law School in 1945 and earned a doctorate in law in 1950. By this time he had become strongly opposed to the United States and its interference in Cuban politics, and he was becoming interested in a career in politics himself. When General Fulgencio Batista staged a coup d'état in 1952, Castro dedicated himself to overthrowing the corrupt dictator. Castro and his supporters attempted to overthrow Batista in 1953 but were unsuccessful; Castro was captured and spent the next two years in prison. While in jail, he read books on political philosophy, military strategy, and history, and he strengthened his determination to overthrow the Cuban government. After his release from prison in 1955, Castro left for Mexico, where he raised a band of guerrilla fighters called the 26th of July Movement after his earlier, failed attempt to overthrow the government. They raised funds, gathered weapons, and trained as fighters, learning the tactics of guerrilla warfare on a ranch near Mexico City and, later, in the mountains in the Sierra Maestra region of eastern Cuba.

to attack the city, a disheartened Batista suddenly fled Cuba on January 1, 1959. Fidel Castro marched into Havana a week later with a band of revolutionaries and began to set up a new government.

After the revolution, Cuba became the only communist country in the Western Hemisphere. In many ways, Castro's regime soon proved to be just as harsh as that of his predecessor. Dissidents were imprisoned, tortured, and even murdered. Those who had supported Batista faced war crimes trials and executions. The new government took over farms and private businesses. Opposition newspapers were shut down, and radio and TV stations were taken over by the government, with their programming consisting of propaganda, trials, and executions. If entertainers wished to continue working, they had to give public support to Castro's regime. Cruz called the situation "unbearable" and said, "Our professional future in Cuba seemed bleak. Freedom of artistic expression did not seem to rank high on the regime's agenda."[22]

THE END OF ARTISTIC FREEDOM

Soon after the revolution, Celia Cruz was performing at a party at the home of Miguel Ángel Quevedo, the publisher of *Bohemia*, which at that time had the highest circulation of any Spanish magazine in the world. While onstage, Cruz realized Fidel Castro was at the party. Quevedo told her that Castro wanted to meet her, saying, "He says that he used to clean his gun to your song 'Burundanga' while he was in the mountains during the insurgency."[23] Cruz, who had no desire to meet Castro, politely responded to Quevedo that he had hired her to perform, and her place was therefore beside the piano.

This situation was repeated the following year, when Cruz performed along with several other bands and singers at Havana's Blanquita Theater. During the rehearsal, the director told all the musicians that Castro would be attending that evening and that everyone was expected to greet him and pay their respects after performing. Again, Castro requested that

When Fidel Castro incited a revolution and seized control of the government, Cuba underwent a transformation. Refusing to allow people to criticize him or his regime, Castro imprisoned and tortured anyone who spoke out against him, including entertainers. Cruz disagreed with Castro and was not safe in Cuba as long as he was in power.

Celia Cruz sing his favorite song, "Burundanga," but Cruz convinced the musicians accompanying her to pretend they did not have the score to the song. Instead, she sang "Cao, Cao, Mani Picao," and when she finished singing, she turned and walked off the stage, completely ignoring Castro, who was sitting in the front row. The director informed Cruz that he could not pay her because she was the only performer who did not show Castro the respect he deserved.

After this incident, Cruz came to a grim realization about the situation in Cuba after the revolution and, in particular, about Fidel Castro. In her autobiography, she explains:

> I realized that by way of his arrogance and despotism, he was destroying all free expression and artistic freedom in Cuba. He had turned what once was beautiful into a weapon to prove how he could control others. As the months passed in that year of 1959, I realized just to what extent he wanted to control everything, and I refused to become another act in his circus. The regime would actually send its agents to fetch me at home to perform at their events. My poor brother, Bárbaro, would answer the door while I hid in an armoire and would tell them I wasn't in Havana. . . . Demons like Castro aren't born, they're made, and they get their strength from manipulating and destroying others.[24]

By publically showing her disapproval of Castro, Celia Cruz was risking her career and possibly even her physical well-being as well, since those who spoke out against the regime could find themselves under arrest. There was also the fact that she needed to continue earning money because her mother had recently been diagnosed with cancer. When Cruz was given a contract to perform for a few months at La Terraza Casino nightclub in Mexico City, she was reluctant to leave her ailing mother, but she needed the work to pay for her mother's medical expenses. Also at that time, the Sonora Matancera was given a contract at the Lírico Theater in Mexico City, and so their director, Rogelio Martínez, set about making travel arrangements and getting permission for both Cruz and the band to travel outside of Cuba—a process that had become much more complex since the revolution.

THE FLIGHT OUT OF CUBA

On the morning of July 15, 1960, Celia Cruz hugged her mother goodbye and assured her she would be home for

Christmas. Tía Ana promised Celia she would take good care of her mother while she was performing in Mexico. At the airport terminal, Celia turned to blow her mother and her aunt a kiss as she walked toward the airplane. Years later, she confided, "I'm glad that I didn't know then that I would never see my mother again. If I'd known, I wouldn't have been able to leave her."[25]

In fact, no one on the airplane knew the truth—with the exception of Rogelio Martínez, who had made the travel arrangements and purchased the airplane tickets. Martínez waited until the airplane had flown out of Cuban airspace, and then he announced that this was to be a one-way trip. Cruz, who would vividly recall the details of that day for the remainder of her life, wrote in her autobiography: "Some of the members of the Sonora began to cry. I remember Pedro having a somber look on his face. He squeezed my hand, and I too began crying. I was struck by the enormity of what I had

LITTLE HAVANA

Celia Cruz and the members of the Sonora Matancera were among the more than 200,000 people who left Cuba for the United States from 1959 to 1962. These exiles created Cuban communities in New York City, northern New Jersey, and Los Angeles, but by far the largest Cuban enclave is in Miami, where more than half of all Cuban Americans live. Here the exiles created what is known as Little Havana, where Spanish is the main language and Cuban restaurants and stores line the main thoroughfare, *Calle de Ocho* (Eighth Street).

One reason Cuban influence remains so strong in Little Havana and the other Cuban communities is that most of the people who fled there believed they would be returning to their homeland soon—as soon as Castro's regime crumbled. As Celia Cruz often said, "I would like to return to Cuba when the present regime is no longer in power."* Like Cruz, most just lost forever. In my heart, I knew I would never see my country again. All I could think of was what I had left behind: my mother, my whole family, and so many friends. My life, as I knew it, was gone."[26]

LIVING IN EXILE

Only one week after the Sonora Matancera went into exile in Mexico, Celia's father, Simón Cruz, died. Celia was heart-broken to learn that she would not be allowed back into the country for her father's funeral. Two years later, when her mother died, Celia again was not allowed to return to her beloved homeland for the funeral, which caused her deep sorrow.

When the orchestra left Cuba, all the members and Celia Cruz were stripped of their Cuban citizenship. In addition, Castro banned their music and had their recordings destroyed in an effort to erase them from Cuba's history. But during the

political refugees from Cuba are very nostalgic about their homeland, and they hold strongly to their roots—including the music they grew up with. Although Castro banned Celia Cruz's music in Cuba, exiles living in places like Little Havana continued to listen to her records. American fashion photographer Bruce Weber commented: "You couldn't walk down a street in Miami during the early 1980s . . . without hearing the music of Celia Cruz pouring out the windows of every second-floor apartment. It was the soundtrack of Miami and I think that's why people fell in love with the city and with the Cuban neighborhood."**

*Quoted in Eduardo Marceles, *Azúcar! The Biography of Celia Cruz.* New York: Reed Press, 2004, p. 107.

**Quoted in Alexis Rodriguez-Duarte, *Presenting Celia Cruz.* New York: Clarkson Potter, 2004, p. 70.

1960s, despite her music being banned in Cuba, Cruz's fame continued to expand throughout the world. She recorded albums with the Sonora Matancera as she began to expand her horizons by working with other, more well-known groups, including Memo Salamanca, with whom she recorded four albums, and with Cuban composer Juan Bruno Tarraza. Her willingness to explore other types of music meant that her work began to appeal to a wider audience. In addition, she toured Mexico with Afro-Mexican singer Toña la Negra, spreading Cuban music in the form of the son and guaracha throughout the country.

A year after the flight out of Cuba, Celia Cruz was given a contract without the Sonora Matancera to perform at the Los Angeles Palladium. While in Los Angeles, she decided to seek asylum in the United States. She felt that the Mexican government was sympathetic to Cuba's communist regime, a situation she found increasingly uncomfortable, since she was an outspoken critic of Fidel Castro. Because of the special consideration the U.S. government gave Cuban refugees at this time, Cruz was able to obtain U.S. citizenship in 1961. However, leaving Mexico was difficult for her because she felt she was once again leaving a place that she had come to think of as home. She took an apartment in New York City, where she was soon reunited with the members of the Sonora Matancera, who had also come to the United States. Cruz continued to sing with the orchestra in their new life in the United States; meanwhile, her personal life was also taking a new direction.

A WEDDING AND A NEW LIFE

Pedro Knight had always felt a special fondness for Celia Cruz, and a close friendship had developed between them over the years. Despite their mutual admiration of one another both personally and professionally, for many years Cruz was not interested in pursuing a serious relationship with him. In fact, when the two of them first met, Knight was a married man with six children; he was divorced a year after Cruz began

Cruz's friendship with musician Pedro Knight blossomed into romance. Knight, Cruz, and other members of the Sonora Matancera defected from Cuba. The couple settled down in the United States and married in 1962.

working with the Sonora Matancera. Still, Cruz would not date Knight because he had a reputation as a ladies' man. In addition, Cruz was briefly engaged to a bass player named Alfredo León during the 1950s. Knight, however, was clearly smitten with the willowy young singer, and he persevered. Paquito

D'Rivera, a Cuban musician and the son of well-known Cuban conductor Tito Rivera, recalls seeing Knight flirt with Cruz onstage back in Cuba in the 1950s: "She used to sing in front of the orchestra, proud, slender, and radiant in her airy linen dresses with white lace, and [Pedro Knight] . . . would blow signs of his affection to her from the trumpet section of the famous Sonora Matancera. He took great pride in Celia, and rightly so, because his girlfriend was already, though very young, the most popular singer in Cuba."[27] Once they settled in the United States, Cruz and Knight began to feel they were the only family they each had. Then, soon after Cruz's mother died, Knight proposed, and at long last Celia Cruz agreed to become his wife. They were married in Connecticut on July 14, 1962.

Soon after they were married, the newlyweds experienced another change in their personal life. Cruz's sister Gladys was very lonely and unhappy in Cuba after the death of Ollita. She was given permission to travel to Mexico in 1963, and from there she sought asylum in the United States. Celia remained very close to Gladys for the rest of her life and loved Gladys's son and two daughters (one of whom was named Celia) as if they were her own children.

In 1965, Celia made a huge decision that would affect the rest of her career. She decided to leave the Sonora Matancera after 15 years of recording with them to pursue a musical career on her own, one in which she could continue to expand her horizons by recording a variety of different styles. Then, in 1967, after more than 20 years of playing trumpet with the Sonora Matancera, Pedro Knight also decided to leave the orchestra to help manage his wife's burgeoning career. Celia Cruz continued to hope that she would return to Cuba some day, once Fidel Castro was overthrown—a day that, sadly, never came for her.

6

The Birth of Salsa

Although Celia Cruz's formal relationship with the Sonora Matancera had ended, she continued to tour with them in Venezuela, Mexico, and the United States throughout the late 1960s and into the 1970s. At the same time, her own musical style was evolving. She had stopped recording with the Sonora because she was tired of singing not only the "same old songs" over and over but also the same style of music again and again. Beginning in the mid- to late 1960s, she began a series of very successful collaborations with other well-known artists. Some of her most successful collaborations come from this period of her career—with Tito Puente, Larry Harlow, Johnny Pacheco, Willie Colón, the Fania All Stars, and others.

It was at this same time that she began to build on the traditional Cuban songs she performed, so that in addition to the usual percussion instruments such as the guiros and conga drums, she was also accompanied by more brass. By the 1970s, she was experimenting with synthesizers, vibraphones, and yet more brass, giving her music a more modern sound. This sound was part of a new style of music called salsa, and Celia Cruz is credited as being one of the musicians responsible for its surge in popularity throughout the world.

TITO PUENTE

In 1966, Cruz began recording with Tito Puente, an artist she admired very much and who would become a lifelong friend of hers. Cruz and Puente met in the 1950s in New York, when he attended a party in her honor. The two spent the evening

SALSA AND ITS QUEEN

Salsa music is derived from many different styles of music, including the son, rumba, guaracha, danzón, and cha-cha-chá, among others. The music also contains elements of merengues from the Dominican Republic and cumbias from Colombia. Even rock, jazz, and the blues have exerted an influence on this hybrid style of music whose name means "spicy sauce." It is no accident that this music, which originated in Cuba and Puerto Rico, came into being in the 1960s, a time that saw a rise in ethnic pride in the United States among blacks, Hispanics, and other groups. Young Hispanics in New York, New Jersey, and Miami caught the salsa fever in the early 1970s.

Salsa music is fast paced and upbeat, making it an ideal dance music. It features intricate rhythms, horn arrangements, and a "scat" and call-and-response aspect. Celia Cruz was excellent at improvising rapid-fire lyrics, and her powerful voice was well suited for keeping up with the quick rhythms. Well-known pioneers of salsa music include Tito Puente, Johnny Pacheco, Rubén Blades, and Willie Colón. In a musical genre dominated by males, Celia Cruz was the only female superstar. More than that, she was the Queen of Salsa, the most loved and most widely recognized salsa performer of all time.

discussing their shared musical interests. Later, when Puente visited Cuba to perform on television, their friendship flourished. In 1965, he called her and asked if she would like to record together, and in 1966, they began a musical collaboration that led to eight albums for Tico Records. Among their early albums were *Celia y Tito* and *Cuba and Puerto Rico Son*. There were some successful singles from each of their albums in the United States and Europe, where people were just beginning to become interested in Caribbean music. One of their biggest hits was called "Acuario," which was their version of "Age of Aquarius" by the Fifth Dimension. The music they performed together is credited with helping to spread the popularity of salsa in the United States and around the world.

Although Cruz and Puente toured all over the world together and were quite successful as a live act, particularly in Japan and the United States, their albums met with only lukewarm commercial success. Cruz felt that the albums did not do well because of a lack of promotion by the recording studio. After recording a total of 12 albums for Tico, 8 of them with Tito Puente, she asked to be released from her contract in 1973.

HOMMY

In that same year, Celia Cruz ventured further into the new genre of salsa by participating in the Latin opera titled *Hommy*. This musical production was based on the 1969 album *Tommy* by the British rock band the Who. The first-ever "rock opera," *Tommy* tells the story of a deaf, mute, and blind boy who likes to play pinball and becomes the leader of a cult. The Who performed their rock opera live many times, most notably at the London Coliseum in 1969 and the Metropolitan Opera House in New York City in 1970.

In 1973, accomplished pianist Larry Harlow composed the salsa version titled *Hommy*, putting the Who's songs to an Afro-Cuban rhythm. He transplanted the original story from London to a Hispanic neighborhood in New York and

Around the time she left the Sonora Matancera, Cruz began experimenting with different musical styles and genres. She collaborated with some of the most talented Latin musicians of that time and even starred in *Hommy*, a Latin version of the rock opera *Tommy* by the Who.

changed the title character's interest in pinball to a love of the bongo. Celia Cruz was cast in the role of Gracia Divina, or Divine Grace. *Hommy* debuted at Carnegie Hall on March 29, 1973, becoming the first Latin musical ever to be performed there, and was performed in Puerto Rico that same year. An

album titled *Hommy: A Latin Opera* was also rel
Cruz singing the same song, "Gracia Divina," tl
sung onstage.

Her performance in the stage production and on the
album for *Hommy* solidified her reputation as a singer with
tremendous skill and professionalism. Larry Harlow recalls
that he had sent her a tape in Mexico so she could learn the
music in order to save time and that when she arrived in New
York to record the song "Gracia Divina" for the album, Cruz
declined his offer of a rehearsal and was able to record the song
in only 20 minutes. Harlow commented on her performance
in the recording studio that day:

> That version on the album was the first and only one that we
> recorded. . . . Celia did not rehearse at all. She sang that song
> from beginning to end, without any mistakes, without having
> to go over anything. . . . I was so surprised that she was ready
> to record right away, without any adjustments. . . . I had never
> seen anyone like that—she's the only one who's done this—
> sing a whole song without rehearsing it, as if she knew my
> orchestra by heart, as if she was inspired.[28]

FANIA ALL STARS

Cruz's association with Larry Harlow would lead her into one
of the most commercially successful phases of her long career.
Harlow recorded on the Fania Record label, which had been
founded in 1963 by Dominican musician Johnny Pacheco and
music promoter Jerry Masucci. Pacheco led a music group
called the Fania All Stars, which featured Harlow on piano.
This group, as its name implies, gathered all the brightest
stars of salsa music to record together, including such legendary musicians as Larry Harlow, Willie Colón, Hector Lavoe,
Johnny Pacheco, Rubén Blades, Eddie Palmieri, Ray Barretto,
and Bobby Valentin. Fania Records is often referred to as the
"Latin Motown," and the Fania All Stars is considered the
most important and influential salsa group ever. After Celia

Cruz left Tico Records, Masucci, impressed by her work on *Hommy*, contacted her and asked her to perform with the Fania All Stars in a concert to be recorded live at Yankee Stadium. This concert in front of 20,000 people was filmed and released in 1974 as *Salsa*, as well as a live, two-album set called *Fania All Stars Live at Yankee Stadium*. Pacheco and Masucci soon signed Cruz to Vaya Records, a subsidiary of Fania Records.

THE FANIA ALL STARS IN AFRICA

After the success of *Salsa*, the Fania All Stars appeared in many other documentaries featuring live performances. One of the most notable of these was filmed in Africa in October 1974, when Celia Cruz performed with Johnny Pacheco and the Fania All Stars in a three-day musical festival. The concert, held before 80,000 fans in Kinshasa, Zaire (now known as the Democratic Republic of the Congo), served as a backdrop to the famous "Rumble in the Jungle" World Heavyweight Championship match between Muhammad Ali and George Foreman. The concert featured many African and American performers, including James Brown, the Pointer Sisters, B.B. King, the Spinners, Sister Sledge, Bill Withers, Miriam "Mama Africa" Makeba, and Manu Dibango. Celia Cruz sang two of her big hits, "Química" and "Guantanamera," and recalled later that she was surprised to discover her Cuban music was so popular in Africa. The concert was filmed by Academy Award–winning director Leon Gast and later released as a movie titled *Celia Cruz and the Fania All Stars in Africa*.

Celia Cruz toured the world with the Fania All Stars: Europe, Africa, North and South America. They spread the popularity of salsa music the world over. Cruz's already considerable fame grew throughout the 1970s as part of this salsa group, because she was exposed to a wider and ever-increasing audience. At the same time, she continued to collaborate with other artists throughout the 1970s. One of the most successful

Cruz's collaborations with musicians like Tito Puente and Johnny Pacheco catapulted her to the top of Latin music. She continued to work with different musical genres and tried rock as well as disco. *Above*, Cruz poses with Tito Puente as he receives a star on the Hollywood Walk of Fame.

of these collaborations brought about one of her most popular albums of all time.

CELIA Y JOHNNY

Once Masucci had signed Celia Cruz to the Vaya label, he asked her who she would like to record an album with. Cruz

A CIRCLE OF FRIENDS

COLLABORATING WITH MORÉ, PUENTE, AND PACHECO

By the 1970s, it was obvious that Celia Cruz was a woman who was rarely content to do only one thing at a time. She would work on a collaboration with one artist, go on tour with another, then return from a world tour to begin a collaboration with yet another. Cruz worked with many different artists in a variety of genres throughout her career, but the three who were perhaps the most influential on her were Benny Moré, Tito Puente, and Johnny Pacheco.

Benny Moré

Early in her career, Cruz collaborated with Benny Moré (1919–1963), a Cuban musician. They first performed together in Cuba in the 1950s. At the time, there was a law that any theater showing a foreign film had to have live performances by Cuban musicians during intermissions, and Moré sang in one of these shows at Havana's Teatro América along with Celia Cruz and Olga Guillot. Moré, who was nicknamed "El Bárbaro del Ritmo," had formed a large orchestra in Cuba. He had a very melodic voice, and Cruz referred to him as one of the greatest Cuban singers ever. Moré died in 1963 at age 44. In 1985, Celia Cruz released an album in his honor, *Homenaje a Beny Moré*, which she recorded with Tito Puente.

Tito Puente

Born in the United States to Puerto Rican parents, Puente was a popular bandleader and musician who was known for his skill on the timbales (drums)—hence his nickname "El Rey de los Timbales" (The Kettledrum

chose Johnny Pacheco because she liked the style of music his band played. Cruz and Pacheco recorded a total of six albums together, which were separate works from those they recorded with the Fania All Stars. They used a format similar to that of the Sonora Matancera, with two trumpets, bass, piano, claves, bongos and timbales, and the tres. Their first album together,

King). Puente grew up listening to Cuban music and helped spread the mambo craze with its big-band style in the United States in the 1950s. His greatest hits included the 1962 song "Oye Como Va" (meaning "Hey, How's It Going"), which would later become a huge hit for the musical group Santana when they recorded their own version in 1970.

Puente once said that *salsa* was just a new name for music that already existed, insisting, "It's the same *mambo* I have been playing for forty years!"* It was while working with Puente and his orchestra that Celia Cruz's music began to take on a big-band sound. Their recordings for Tico Records helped bring Cruz international attention.

Johnny Pacheco

Like Benny Moré and Tito Puente, Johnny Pacheco was a well-known bandleader, composer, and arranger. Pacheco is Dominican; he moved to New York City with his family when he was 12. His father was a bandleader and a clarinetist. Johnny Pacheco learned to play the flute, violin, saxophone, clarinet, and accordion, and he studied percussion at the prestigious Juilliard School of Music. He formed his first orchestra, Pacheco y Su Charanga, in 1960; an album by the same name sold more than 100,000 copies. He cofounded Fania Records with Jerry Mascucci in 1963, but the company had trouble competing with the already successful and well-established record labels of the time. Pacheco did not give up, going so far as to deliver records to stores in his own car. In 1968, he organized the best salsa musicians from the label into a new group called the Fania All Stars. He again lent his flavor to Celia Cruz's music in 2001 when he helped produce her album *La Negra Tiene Tumbao (The Black Woman Has Rhythm)*.

*Quoted in Eduardo Marceles, *Azúcar! The Biography of Celia Cruz.* New York: Reed Press, 2004, p. 133.

released in 1974, was titled simply *Celia y Johnny*. This album enjoyed great commercial success, going gold, and introduced the hit song "Químbara." Cruz has said that of all the albums she recorded, the two she was proudest of were *Reflexiones*, which she recorded with the Sonora Matancera, and *Celia y Johnny*. This gold record included several songs that became huge hits, including "Canto a La Habana," "Químbara," and "Toro Mata," an Afro-Peruvian rhythm Cruz first heard during a visit to South America.

Although by this time it had been 14 years since Celia Cruz had fled Cuba, her love for her homeland was still obvious in the lyrics of *Celia y Johnny*. The song "Canto a La Habana," or "Ode to Havana," became an unofficial anthem for Cubans in exile, with lyrics that clearly illustrate their pain at living away from their homeland:

> Oh, your landscape is beautiful
> Beautiful Cuba, beautiful Cuba
> You are so beautiful
> Oh, your landscape is beautiful
> My Cuba, I cry for you
> Little Cuba, I yearn for you.[29]

PERSONAL LIFE

As popular and famous as she was the world over, Celia Cruz was very protective of her private life. She and Pedro Knight were inseparable; he was her musical director and traveled everywhere she went, standing just offstage at all her performances and sometimes even appearing onstage with her during a song. They were very much in love and deeply committed to one another. During this period of their lives, Cruz and Knight discussed the possibility of having children. Cruz adored children and believed that if she became a mother, she would want to retire in order to provide her children with some stability in their lives. Knight also loved children—in fact, he already had seven children from two previous marriages. Sadly, however, Celia was not able to become pregnant, in spite of undergoing several expensive fertility treatments. Even though she and Knight did not have children of their own, they doted on their nieces and nephews, particularly the son and two daughters of Cruz's sister Gladys who had come to live in the United States. In addition, Cruz and Knight "adopted" children all over the world, keeping photograph albums and maintaining correspondences. The two of them helped christen more than 50 children over the years. Later in life, Cruz reflected that because of all the love she shared with these children, she was at peace with the fact that she was unable to have children of her own.

Celia Cruz had already lived a very full life, recording traditional Cuban music as well as the new genre of salsa, and even venturing into disco by the end of the 1970s. Yet she showed no signs of slowing down or of wanting to "take things easy" at this point in her life. As busy as she was in the 1970s as the Queen of Salsa, however, it seemed this world-renowned performer was just getting warmed up. As she ventured into the 1980s, her career diversified as she reinvented herself yet again, branching out into other genres and other mediums as well.

7

Branching Out

Fania Records had reigned supreme in the 1970s, but by the end of the decade, other Latin music labels had sprung up to challenge Fania's monopoly. There were financial problems, too, and some artists were dissatisfied by what they saw as low pay for their work. By 1980, cofounder Jerry Masucci had left the company; several artists followed suit, including Willie Colón and Rubén Blades.

With Fania Records now in decline, the artists involved in the Fania All Stars began going their various ways. Of all of them, Celia Cruz seemed to be the one whose career star continued to shine the brightest. Beginning in the early 1980s, Cruz made appearances seemingly everywhere, including small New York City nightclubs; large stadiums all over the United States; open-air plazas in Spain, Colombia, and Mexico; and even guest starring on American television. The world just could not seem to get enough of the Queen of

Salsa, and her popularity continued to soar throughout the decade.

A NEW DECADE

True to her indomitable spirit, Celia Cruz kicked off the 1980s in style. While some of the other artists who had been part of Fania may have experienced a slump in their careers or even slipped into obscurity, such was not the case for the

CELIA CRUZ IN CONCERT

Celia Cruz in concert was truly an amazing spectacle. There was absolutely no one else who could compare with her anywhere in the world. Sue Steward, an author and television producer, provides an apt description of the Queen of Salsa in action:

> In person, Celia Cruz emits a contagious glow; on stage it bursts into full flame. Her performances are a whirl of movement and joyfulness, feet and hips twisting and shimmying, reflecting light-beams off her outrageous costumes and Tiffany jewels. Her penetrating voice, with its operatic range and sure, sophisticated sense of timing, her computer-fast improvisations and fast, playful onomatopoeic scats are exceptional by any standards. Even her trademark catchline—a barking call "Azúcaaaaar!" (Sugar!)—brings on goose-bumps. All her skills are exercised in the finale to her shows, "Bemba colorá" (Thick Red Lips), in which she sings, with feigned humility:
>
> > Don't forget the name of this poor singer,
> > I've worn my best dress,
> > I've given all I can. . .
> > My name is *Celia Cruz.*[*]

*Sue Steward, *Música! Salsa, Rumba, Merengue, and More.* San Francisco: Chronicle, 1999, p. 59.

Queen of Salsa. In 1980, she received the New York Music Award for Best Latin Artist, as well as her fourth Grammy nomination, for *Eternos*, which she recorded with Johnny Pacheco. During the 1980s, she also toured in Latin America and Europe many times, performing in multiple concerts wherever she went.

By this time, Celia Cruz was drawing enormous crowds whenever and wherever she performed. In 1987, she performed at the Carnaval de Santa Cruz de Tenerife in Spain in front of an audience of 250,000 people. This performance earned her a spot in the *Guinness Book of World Records* for the largest audience ever recorded at a concert.

Cruz continued to collaborate with numerous artists during the 1980s and 1990s. She recorded an album titled *Celia y Willie* with Willie Colón in 1981. In 1982, she sang with the Sonora Matancera for the first time in 17 years to produce the album *Feliz Encuentro* (*Happy Reunion*). The album was followed by a huge celebration commemorating the seventy-fifth anniversary of the Sonora Matancera, at which Cruz performed some of the greatest hits she had recorded with the orchestra, including "Guantanamera," "Bembé Colorá," and "La Bella Cubana."

By 1985, Celia Cruz was 60 years old, but she showed no signs of slowing down and continued to tour and record at a frantic pace. More collaborations would follow, including those with Willy Chirino, Gloria Estefan, La India, Tito Puente, and Johnny Pacheco. In 1987, Vaya Records released Celia's 53rd album, titled *The Winners*, another collaboration with her old friend Willie Colón. In 1989, she recorded the song "Obladi Oblada" in Spanish with Tito Puente on the album *Tropical Tribute to the Beatles*. The song, which is based on a 1968 song by the Beatles, became a big hit for Cruz and Puente. Also in 1989, she recorded *Ritmo en el Corazón* with master conga player Ray Barreto, for which they shared a Grammy Award. It was her first Grammy, although she had been nominated numerous times before.

SOMETHING NEW

Celia Cruz branched out musically during the 1980s by collaborations with non-Hispanic musicians, including Patti LaBelle, Dionne Warwick, and David Byrne of the Talking Heads. In 1986, she recorded the single "Loco de Amor" with Byrne for the opening scene of the box-office hit film *Something Wild*, starring Melanie Griffith. It was an unusual collaboration, because their singing styles were so vastly different—where she was spirited and vivacious, he was dead-pan and understated. Byrne, however, had synthesized African rhythms into the music of the Talking Heads, and he had been a fan of hers for years. He asked the producers of the movie if he could do the song "Loco de Amor," which was cowritten by Johnny Pacheco, as a duet with her, and they agreed.

DISCO AND HIP-HOP

In the late 1970s, Cruz had ventured into disco when she recorded the hit songs "Spanish Fever," "Desafio," and "Ella Fue" with the Fania All Stars. Throughout the 1980s and beyond, she continued in this vein of lending her voice to different styles of music. In 1997, she sang with former Fugees member Wyclef Jean on his hip-hop album *The Carnival*. They earned a Grammy Award nomination for Best Rap Performance for the song "Guantanamera" from the album. The successful collaboration with Jean exposed millions of hip-hop fans around the world to the unique voice of Celia Cruz.

In 2000, Cruz did a remake on her album *Siempre Viviré* of the 1970s disco classic "I Will Survive" by Gloria Gaynor. Another big hit would follow in 2002, when Cruz was nearing her eightieth birthday—her last big hit, "La Negra Tiene Tumbao," from the album by the same name. This song blends tropical sounds with hip-hop. In the video for the song, she wore a bright orange wig, prompting columnist Lydia Martin to comment: "Celia may have been Old Cuba, but she was as hip as MTV."[30]

In the 1980s, Cruz was an established, popular Latin recording artist. She continued to collaborate with other musicians in different genres, like Patti LaBelle and David Byrne of the Talking Heads.

BRINGING SALSA TO THE SCREEN

During her many tours of Latin America in the 1980s, Celia Cruz made guest appearances on television shows in many of the countries she visited. These appearances increased her already considerable popularity in those countries, particularly Mexico, Colombia, and Venezuela. Later in the decade, Cruz was delighted to appear on American television when she was invited by one of the creators of *Sesame Street* to perform on the venerable children's show. In 1989, she sang "Sun Sun Ba Baé," which had been a big hit for her back in Cuba in the 1950s, as a duet with Big Bird. In 1994, she was invited back to *Sesame Street*, and she sang two more of her big hits, "Burundanga" and "Químbara," which she performed with the Muppets. These appearances introduced thousands of young American children—as well as their parents—to the Queen of Salsa and her music.

Cruz also ventured onto the silver screen when she began appearing in small roles beginning in the late 1980s. She had already appeared in a few movies in the 1950s in Cuba, always playing herself onstage with the Sonora Matancera in scenes with a band playing in the background for nightclub shows or parties. She had appeared in numerous documentaries during the 1970s with the Fania All Stars—essentially concerts that were filmed live—including the documentaries *Salsa* and *Celia Cruz and the Fania All Stars in Africa*. In 1988, she appeared as herself in her first Hollywood movie, also titled *Salsa*, which starred Robby Rosa. The movie was billed as a Latin version of the disco-driven *Saturday Night Fever*, starring John Travolta. In *Salsa*, the main character sets out to win a salsa dancing contest in order to better his life. The movie did not do well at the box office, but it did help to broaden Celia Cruz's audience and increase the popularity of salsa music in the United States.

A STYLE REVOLUTION

Celia Cruz had a talent for "reinventing" herself over and over during her career as her musical style and fashion sense were continually evolving. She liked to change with the times, and she reinvented herself many times. This ability to adapt to a variety of musical styles was part of the reason she was so successful for so many years.

In addition to changing her musical tastes, she also constantly updated her appearance, keeping pace with the fashions

Throughout her career, Cruz was known for having a very distinctive look. When she was with the Sonora Matancera, she was slender, with straightened hair, but as her solo career flourished, she began to wear colorful wigs and dress in flamboyant clothes.

of the day. In the 1950s, she wore her straightened hair in a sleek bun or braid, or sometimes under a turban, which were all popular styles in that decade. Early in her career, her figure was quite slender, and she cut an elegant pose in the form-fitting gowns of the time. In the early 1960s, her style was still somewhat conservative, but by later in the decade, she was starting to evolve into her eventual flamboyant style onstage. She also embraced her African heritage by wearing caftans and big Afro wigs in the 1960s and 1970s. She dressed with the times and also with the style of music she was doing at the time. Her personal style was always a reflection of the fashion and music of the times.

Her style evolved once again, along with her music, as she dressed in the disco fashions of the late 1970s and early 1980s. She wore lots of makeup, glittery dresses with shoulder pads, and wigs with elaborate hairdos. By this time in her life, her figure had matured from that of a skinny young girl to a voluptuous woman, and she embraced her full, feminine curves with costumes that showed them off when she danced to the music onstage.

In the 1990s, her style continued to evolve, but it was always flamboyant. She wore wigs in all colors—platinum, orange, purple—and always inch-long, painted fingernails. Guillermo Cabrere Infante, a Cuban writer living in exile in London, once commented on Celia Cruz's remarkable fashion sense: "Celia's good humor was expressed in her wardrobe, full of multicolored costumes, usually topped by a striking wig, which she wore like another hat. It was not a caricature, like the hats brimming with fruit worn by Carmen Miranda, but just another manifestation of her humor. The exaggerated makeup was also festive: the enormous mouth, the heavy eyelashes, the eyebrows like circumflex accent marks were all humorous."[31]

As flamboyant as she was onstage, these outfits were merely her stage dress—costumes. When she was not performing, she dressed more conservatively, wearing modest dresses

FLYING SHOES

Of all the style motifs for which Celia Cruz was known, none perhaps could match the marvel of her "flying shoes." These platform shoes were custom-made for her by a Mexican shoemaker named Mr. Nieto. They were reinforced with steel and included a four-inch-tall, recessed heel, which helped give the illusion onstage that she was constantly on her toes. A pair of these shoes is now on display at the Smithsonian, along with a red and white polka-dot dress from one of her performances. Cuban-born Alexis Rodriguez-Duarte, who fled his native country in 1968 with his parents, photographed Celia Cruz numerous times over the years. He commented on her shoes:

> I thought that Celia's shoes were a true testament to her style. Those four-inch heels made of steel were an architectural marvel, so I asked Celia if she wouldn't mind lifting up her skirt a little so I could photograph them. At first she looked shocked and said, "Ay . . . don't photograph my legs, I don't have pretty legs!" But when I explained that I wanted to photograph her shoes, she said, "Fine, O.K.," and lifted her skirt. Years later she told me that I was the only person who ever photographed her shoes with such an attention to detail.
>
> What's fascinating about these shoes is that they were all made by one particular shoemaker she discovered in Mexico City in the late 1950s or early 1960s. Once she started wearing them, they became the only shoes she would perform in. After the shoemaker died in the 1970s, Celia found other shoemakers in Los Angeles and Miami to keep refurbishing them.[*]

*Alexis Rodriguez-Duarte, *Presenting Celia Cruz.* New York: Clarkson Potter, 2004, p. 20.

or suits and pulling her dark hair back into a sleek bun. Her personal style was in stark contrast to her onstage costumes, some of which cost more to produce than her albums. In the late 1980s, Cruz was obliged to tone her costumes down a bit, as she explained to a *New York Times* reporter: "Sometimes my gowns were longer or wider than the stage. Duets were the worst; my partners either couldn't stand close enough to me, like you should when doing a romantic duet, or they'd get feathers in their faces."[32]

PERSONAL TRIUMPHS

When Celia Cruz and Pedro Knight married in 1962, they had a civil ceremony with a Connecticut judge presiding. They both had wanted a church wedding, but this had not been possible, because neither of them could produce their baptism certificates, which were back in Cuba. None of the members of the Sonora Matancera had brought such records with them, because none of them knew their flight out of Cuba that day was to be a one-way trip. After they left, the government would not allow their baptism certificates to be sent out of the country.

In 1987, with their twenty-fifth wedding anniversary approaching, the couple talked about renewing their vows in a church ceremony, but they were afraid it would still be impossible. Three churches declined to perform the ceremony without the baptism certificates before they finally found a priest who agreed to marry them in a Catholic service. With 300 friends and family members in attendance, this was an especially touching moment for Cruz and Knight, because when they had first married, they did not have much money, their ceremony had been quite simple, and they had never taken a honeymoon. The two of them both considered the picture they had taken that day to be their official wedding portrait.

In 1990, Cruz and Knight experienced another personal triumph. After decades of living in hotel rooms and rented apartments in Mexico, the United States, and other countries all over the world, Cruz and Knight bought their first home together. This townhouse in Fort Lee, New Jersey, was truly a home befitting a queen. It had four floors and an elevator with a telephone inside it. An interior patio was filled with white orchids, and a garage housed four cars. A library held a piano and numerous trophies, awards, keys to cities, and other honors bestowed upon Celia Cruz. She and Knight were very happy in the townhouse, and they lived there until the final months of her life.

8

Awards and Accolades

In April 1989, Celia Cruz was invited to perform at a Cuban exile event at the White House. She sang the Cuban national anthem before hundreds of officials and special guests, including President George H.W. Bush, Vice President Dan Quayle, and Cuban exile leaders. It was a proud moment for her, but also a poignant one, as thoughts of the country she was forced to flee filled her mind. Years later, she would still recall the knot she felt in her throat as she sang the anthem before all those important people.

She had come a long way from the days when she sang for cakes in radio contests back in Havana. Along the way, she had met several U.S. presidents. She met with President Ronald Reagan several times during the 1980s and felt a special fondness for him. In 1994, President Bill Clinton awarded her the National Endowment for the Arts' National Medal of Arts on the White House South Lawn. The medal is the highest honor

79

given to artists in the United States. In 1998, Clinton again honored Cruz by presenting her with the Hispanic Heritage Lifetime Achievement Award. She would meet President George H.W. Bush again, too, at the commencement ceremony of Florida International University, which had awarded her an honorary doctorate—her second. Her first honorary doctorate was from Yale in May 1989; at the commencement ceremony, she received a standing ovation when her name was called. A third honorary doctorate would follow, from the University of Panama, and a fourth, from the University of Miami. With so many honors to her name, it seemed there was little this vibrant woman could not do.

THE ACTING BUG

During the 1990s, Celia Cruz again turned to the screen to try her hand at acting. She had already made small appearances in several films and documentaries by this time, always playing herself. In the early 1990s, however, she began to appear in films as an actress playing a role. The first of these was 1992's *Mambo Kings*, starring Armand Assante and Antonio Banderas in his Hollywood debut. Her character, a black santera named Evalina Montoya, owned a nightclub called Club Babalu in New York. This character did not appear in the novel on which the movie was based, but the producer of the movie was a Celia Cruz fan and decided to create a part for her. Her old friend Tito Puente also appeared in a small role in the film, playing himself.

The film is primarily in English, although there are a few scenes in Spanish with English subtitles toward the beginning. However, Celia's speaking parts—as well as her songs—are completely in English. Although she understood and could speak English, she was not entirely fluent, and she spoke with a heavy Cuban accent. A diction coach was brought in to work with her, as well as with Spaniard Antonio Banderas, who had to learn his lines phonetically. Cruz ended up being very pleased with her performance in English, as well as her songs,

"La Dicha Mia," "Guantanamera," and "Melao de Caña." *The Mambo Kings* enjoyed some box office success, and with its release, Celia Cruz reached the height of her popularity in the United States.

Celia Cruz followed up her success in *The Mambo Kings* by making a cameo appearance in the 1995 film *The Perez Family*, starring Marisa Tomei, Alfred Molina, and Anjelica Huston. The film was based on a novel written by Christine Bell. *The Perez Family* tells the story of a group of unrelated Cuban refugees living in America who pretend to be a family. Cruz plays the part of Luz Pat, a santera whom the family consults for advice. Initially filmed in 11 scenes, the character played by Cruz wound up in only 3 scenes after editing. The movie did not do as well at the box office as *The Mambo Kings*, but Cruz was grateful for the opportunity to appear in another Hollywood film.

In the early 1990s, Cruz appeared in a Latin soap opera titled *El Alma No Tiene Color*, which was well received in

THE MAMBO KINGS PLAY SONGS OF LOVE

The movie *Mambo Kings* that Celia Cruz appeared in alongside Antonio Banderas and Armand Assante was based on a novel by Oscar Hijuelos. Titled *The Mambo Kings Play Songs of Love*, the novel tells the story of two Cuban brothers, Cesar and Nestor Castillo, who immigrate to the United States in the 1950s. The brothers, musicians, settle in New York City and form a mambo band, eventually appearing on the TV show *I Love Lucy* with their hero, Desi Arnaz (who was brilliantly portrayed in the movie version by his son, Desi Arnaz Jr.). The novel received a Pulitzer Prize in 1990, making Hijuelos, who was born in New York City to Cuban immigrant parents, the first Hispanic to receive a Pulitzer Prize for Fiction. In addition to spawning a Hollywood movie in 1992, the novel was also turned into a musical in 2005.

Cruz's music influenced so many that President Bill Clinton awarded her the National Medal of Arts in 1994. *Above*, Cruz attends the ceremony with fellow recipients, actor-singer Harry Belafonte (*left*) and jazz musician Dave Brubeck (*center*).

Mexico. She was then asked to perform in another soap opera in Mexico titled *Valentina*. She liked the idea of doing another acting role in her native language, so she and Pedro Knight flew to Mexico for the filming in 1997. Cruz played a clairvoyant who was the mother of a santera, a role she was by now quite familiar with and which she later recalled felt comfortable to her. Her role in *Valentina* was enormously popular in Mexico and Latin America; later the soap opera was broadcast around the world and was even dubbed into Russian.

A LONG LIST OF HONORS

During the final years of her life, Celia Cruz received so many awards and honors that it would be impossible to name all of them in a short space. She was immortalized in wax at the

Hollywood Wax Museum. She was given keys to the cities of New York; San Francisco; Miami; Orlando; Dallas; Mérida, Mexico; and Lima, Peru. She received a star on both the Hollywood Walk of Fame and the Miami Walk of Fame; she is also featured in Venezuela's Walk of Fame in Caracas, Mexico's Galeria Walk of Fame in Mexico City, and Costa Rica's Walk of Fame in San José. The mayors of Miami and Union City, New Jersey, named streets in her honor—the legendary Calle de Ocho in Little Havana is now known as Celia Cruz Way. A street was also named after her in Spain. She was honored at the 1995 New Orleans Jazz Festival; in 1997, October 25 became Celia Cruz Day in San Francisco.

In 1999, the American Society of Composers, Authors and Publishers presented her with the Award of Herencia Latina, one of its most prestigious awards, for her contributions to spreading Latin music to listeners around the world.

GUANTÁNAMO BAY

In 1990, Celia Cruz was invited to sing at the U.S. naval base at Guantánamo Bay for the Cuban refugees held there. She recalled years later that she cried for several days after receiving the invitation, because she was so moved to be able to visit her beloved homeland, even though she would not be allowed off the base. After 30 years in exile, it was an exciting and yet sad experience for her and Pedro Knight, who accompanied her on the trip. When the military plane landed and they disembarked, Cruz, overcome with emotion, knelt and kissed the ground three times. She then approached the border fence, topped with barbed wire, and put her hand through the chain links to the Cuban side to grab a handful of soil. It was the closest she ever came to returning to the country of her birth. She kept that small, plastic pouch of soil for the remainder of her life, instructing her husband to bury her with it if she should die before Cuba became free.

She is the recipient of two Desi Awards, which recognize the achievements of Hispanics in film, television, and music; in 1992, she won a Desi for Favorite Film Actress for her role in *The Mambo Kings*, and in 1995, she won a Desi Lifetime Achievement Award. Cruz also received the Ellis Island Medal of Honor, the Hispanic Women Achievers Award, the Hispanic Heritage Lifetime Achievement Award, and the Smithsonian Institution Lifetime Achievement Award. In 2001, the Smithsonian also presented her with one of its

BEING HISPANIC

THE SOUND OF CUBA IN CELIA CRUZ'S VOICE

On June 18, 1962, Celia Cruz became the first Hispanic woman to perform at New York City's famous Carnegie Hall. She recalled in her autobiography that this was one of her proudest accomplishments in life. She was always fiercely proud of her Hispanic heritage and particularly of her Cuban roots. It is for this reason that of all the nicknames she earned, *La Guarachera de Cuba* was her favorite.

Wherever she went in life, she carried her love of Cuba and its music with her. Early in her career, she performed in many traditional Afro-Cuban styles, including bolero, calypso, chachachá, conga, cumbia, danzón, guaguancó, guajira, guaracha, mambo, merengue, montuno, porro, rumba, and son. Even when she explored many other styles of music throughout her life, the music of Cuba always had an influence on her performance.

The evidence of her connection to the Cuban music she grew up with can be seen in the fact that this 10-time Grammy nominee sang only in Spanish, even as she continued to gain popularity in the United States and the rest of the English-speaking world. Singing only in Spanish tended to limit her marketability in the United States; but with the arrival of salsa music in the late 1960s, she enjoyed a surge of popularity the world over. Cruz admitted that she might have seen greater success in the mainstream music scene in America if she had sung in English. The reason she gave for not doing so was that, because highest honors, the James Smithson Medal, saying it was "in recognition of her contributions to the increase and diffusion of knowledge."[33] *Billboard* magazine also presented her with a Lifetime Achievement Award and in 2000 featured her smiling picture on the cover of a special issue dedicated to her in honor of her fiftieth anniversary onstage. In 2001, a wonderful opportunity arose when she was invited to sing her longtime hit "Guantanamera" with Luciano Pavarotti onstage in Modena, Italy.

she was less fluent in English, it would have limited her spontaneity onstage. She was well known for her improvisational style—on 1974's *Fania All Stars Live at Yankee Stadium*, she performed a 20-minute-long improvisation of her famous hit song "Bemba Colorá" that left the audience breathless—and singing in English would have meant performing each song exactly the way she had memorized it. She preferred to be able to improvise lyrics on the spur of the moment in her native tongue, and so she stuck with Spanish. David Byrne of the Talking Heads, who recorded a duet with Cruz in 1986, was especially impressed by her extraordinary skill as a singer. After her death, he spoke about her ability to convey her Cuban roots just by the sound of her voice and about how she embraced Cuban musical traditions even when recording in different genres.

Celia Cruz could represent a whole attitude and way of life with just one note. The sound of her voice told you more than a thousand books or pictures—in it you could sense the cuisine, the dancing, the clothes, the humor, sadness, and soul of a whole culture. In one voice you could hear millions. Her voice embodied sensuality, pleasure, melancholy and spirituality—all at the same time. And her decision, with Pedro, to always remain true to her music and sound while still changing with the times was an example to us all.*

*Quoted in Alexis Rodriguez-Duarte, *Presenting Celia Cruz.* New York: Clarkson Potter, 2004, p. 37.

One honor that Cruz found especially heartwarming was being named grand marshal of the National Puerto Rican Day Parade along New York City's Fifth Avenue in 1988. She had first performed in Puerto Rico in 1952 and had always felt a special fondness for the country's people and music, incorporating elements of Puerto Rican music and dance into her own. Another honor that she found highly touching was being asked to perform at the reinauguration of the Freedom Tower in Miami. The tower is where hundreds of thousands of Cubans who had fled their homeland after the revolution were processed as refugees when they entered the United States, and it holds a special significance for all Cuban Americans. Years later, the Freedom Tower would be draped with a giant Cuban flag when Celia Cruz lay in state there after her death.

One of the highest honors she received was awarded to her posthumously. In 2003, a bill was introduced to award Celia Cruz a Congressional Gold Medal. This is the highest civilian award in the United States. Among the reasons Congress stated for awarding her the medal were:

> While best known for her work as an entertainer, Celia Cruz influenced the lives of millions of people as an ambassador of Latino culture and a powerful voice of freedom. . . .
>
> Celia Cruz was much more than just a singer to millions of fans worldwide, especially to Latinos in America, and her contributions to music, Latino culture, and American society make her most deserving of America's highest civilian award, the Congressional Gold Medal.[34]

GRAMMY AWARDS

During her career, Celia Cruz had 23 gold albums and was nominated for 10 Grammy Awards, of which she won 7. In 1990, she won her first Grammy, for Best Tropical Latin Performance, which she shared with Ray Baretto for their album *Ritmo en el Corazón* (*Rhythm in the Heart*). Beginning in 2000, she won back-to-back Grammy Awards every year.

After 50 years in the entertainment business, Cruz's boundless energy and work ethic made her one of the most famous Cubans in the world and earned her numerous awards and honors. *Above*, Cruz poses with her Grammy for Best Salsa Album in 2003.

First was a Latin Grammy for Best Salsa Performance for her album *Celia Cruz and Friends: A Night of Salsa*, followed in 2001 by a Latin Grammy for Best Tropical Traditional Album for *Siempre Viviré* (I Will Survive). In 2002, she won a Latin Grammy for Best Salsa Album for *La Negra Tiene Tumbao* (The Black Lady Has Rhythm/Attitude), which also won a Grammy Award for Best Salsa album in 2003. The last album she recorded, *Regalo del Alma* (Gift from My Soul), likewise won two Grammys: a 2003 Grammy for Best Salsa/Merengue and a posthumous 2004 Latin Grammy for Best Salsa Album.

NOTHING HELD HER BACK

Celia Cruz was not one to slow down. In fact, in 1987, at age 62—an age when many people are thinking of retirement—she told a *New York Times* reporter: "I have a lot more to do."[35] Cruz had toured the world, given concerts, made public appearances, and recorded tirelessly. Indeed, she recorded more than 100 albums and several hundred songs throughout her long career. She always had a happy, broad smile on her face and an optimistic outlook on life and never wanted anyone to know she was ill or in pain. Toward the end of her life, she kept her spirits up, even when her health began to fail. Alexis Rodriguez-Duarte, who photographed Cruz numerous times over the years, recalled a photo session with her one day in which her knees were paining her. Despite her discomfort, she continued with the photo shoot and worked for six hours straight, not even breaking for lunch. Soon afterward, she had knee surgery, and her doctor told her to stop wearing her trademark high heels (advice that she cheerfully ignored). It seemed that nothing could hold her back from her true calling. The Queen of Salsa, *La Guarachera de Cuba*, kept singing and recording right up to the very end of her life.

9

The Death of an Icon

When Celia Cruz appeared at the Grammy Awards in February 2003 wearing a flowing gown and looking the part of a real queen, no one except her husband and a handful of close friends knew just how seriously ill she really was. She had undergone several operations in the past few months, but still her fans had no idea that she was gravely ill. There was a mastectomy in September 2002 that was kept very confidential, because Cruz did not want her fans to pity her. After the mastectomy, she began to experience frequent headaches, along with fainting spells and shivering. Doctors in New York discovered that she had a brain tumor, and in December 2002, she underwent surgery to remove it. Early in 2003, she also had surgery on a knee that had been troubling her for years.

Through it all, she kept her spirits, and she was as cheerful as always. She had been through three surgeries in four months—first the mastectomy, then the brain surgery,

89

followed closely by the knee surgery, but she and those around her were optimistic that *La Guarachera de Cuba* would recover as always. It was a shock to everyone when the pathology results showed that her tumor was malignant. In addition, doctors found three more brain tumors that turned out to be inoperable.

GIFT FROM MY SOUL

That spring, Celia Cruz recorded what was to be her last album, *Regalo del Alma* (*Gift from My Soul*). In the recording studio, she was so weak from chemotherapy that she had to record each line one at a time, but she never complained. Her indomitable spirit remained right up to the end. Later, she would experience confusion onstage when she forgot the words to a song at an event held in her honor in Miami, but she recovered with her usual grace and self-composure, saying, "I want to thank God first, because when I got *la malanga esa* (that whatchamacallit), it did not do away with me, I am still here."[36]

Her final public appearance was on April 2, 2003, at a benefit in New York. The ravages of her illness were evident in her gaunt physical appearance and in her faint voice. For the first time ever, she had to read her lyrics as she sang. After this appearance, her condition went downhill quickly, both physically and mentally. By the time her brother Bárbaro died on May 6, 2003, Celia Cruz was nearly comatose at her home in Fort Lee. She had given up hope that the chemotherapy would help her improve and had stopped her treatments entirely. On her forty-first wedding anniversary, July 14, 2003, she awoke briefly to find her beloved Pedro kneeling beside the bed. He asked her if she knew what day it was, which brought tears to her eyes; before long, however, she had slipped back into unconsciousness.

Celia Cruz died two days later.

REMEMBERING CELIA CRUZ

In her autobiography, Celia Cruz commented that she viewed death as "just a temporary separation," adding, "We will meet

When Cruz died in 2003, her death affected many people, including the musicians and recording artists she had influenced in her long career. An estimated 50,000 people attended her New York funeral and stood in the street to bid their farewells as a horse-drawn carriage carried her coffin away.

again in the afterlife."[37] Her death affected thousands of people around the world, but none so much as her constant companion of more than 40 years, Pedro Knight. Standing beside Knight at her deathbed was longtime friend Johnny Pacheco, who had become so emotional when the priest delivered the last rites that he had to leave the room. Pacheco recalled that when Cruz passed away, Knight turned to him and said, "I want to die." Pacheco replied, "Pedro, you cannot die now."[38] Although Knight lived another three and a half years, until February 2007, he was but a shadow of his former self, lost in a sea of pain, confusion, and sadness.

Johnny Pacheco commented after her death: "Celia shone with her own light, God gave her that light, that very special gift I was lucky enough to share for so many years. Celia was my sister, my companion, and my *Diosa Divina* (Divine Goddess). With her voice, and the humility of a great lady, she stole everybody's hearts. There will never be anybody else like her."[39]

Others who were close to her would feel the pain of her passing, as well, and they remembered her with tremendous fondness. Marc Anthony and his wife, Jennifer Lopez, were particularly close to Cruz. Lopez said: "Now that she is gone, the music world feels empty, devoid of an energy, a life force that drove us, inspired us and made our lives better. Her voice her presence will always be missed . . . but her music will live on forever."[40]

Cuban immigrant Lydia Martin, a columnist with the *Miami Herald*, sums up: "Celia was *son*. She was *salsa*. She was the music that reached our very core, even when our core went wandering toward new languages and new rhythms. She was

SALSA LOSES THREE LEGENDS

Celia Cruz was the third major salsa star to die within a week. Compay Segundo was a Cuban guitarist and composer who was part of Los Compadres, one of the most successful Cuban duos of the 1940s and 1950s. Segundo played on 1997's *Buena Vista Social Club*, which gathered together Cuban musicians who had been largely unknown outside the country until the album's release. He passed away in Havana at the age of 95 on July 13, 2003. On that same day, Tito Duarte, a Cuban-born composer, singer, and instrumentalist, died in Spain while working on a show titled "Dreams Come and Go" for the world-famous guitar festival in Córdoba. He was the son of the legendary Cuban pianist and composer Ernesto Duarte and had moved to Spain with his family as a teenager but continued to embrace his Cuban roots through his music.

the essence of *azúcar*. And the soul of congas that have been pounding since ancestral times."[41]

CELIA CRUZ'S MUSICAL LEGACY

In 2005, the book *Guinness World Records* listed Celia Cruz as the artist with the longest working career as a salsa artist. Over the course of her career, she influenced countless other musicians with her unique style. Among these is Cuban-born Gloria Estefan, whose family fled after the revolution when she was only a toddler. Estefan got her start singing with the Miami Sound Machine in the 1980s. She and her husband, music producer Emilio Estefan, both became close friends with Cruz and Knight.

Marc Anthony idolized Cruz as a singer. One of the proudest moments of his career came in 2001, when he sang "Químbara" with Celia Cruz at a Radio City Music Hall concert.

Another artist who has been strongly influenced by Cruz is Puerto Rican–born La India, known for singing hip-hop and salsa. In 1996, she sang a duet with Celia Cruz titled "La Voz de la Experienca" ("The Voice of Experience"); Cruz subsequently dubbed La India the Princess of Salsa. Mexican-American singer Selena, who rose to stardom as the Queen of Tejano Music before being murdered in 1995 by the president of her own fan club, was also influenced by the musical style of Celia Cruz.

Part of her musical legacy is lending her voice to the documentary *La Cuba Mía (My Cuba)* with Spanish musician Miliki, who had been popular in both Cuba and Spain. The documentary, which was made during the last few months of Cruz's life, explored popular Cuban music in the twentieth century, and no one could have been better suited as cohost than *La Guarachera de Cuba* herself.

Cuban-born singer Lucrecia, who lives in exile in Spain, has been called by many the successor to Celia Cruz. Here, Lucrecia sums up the reason for Celia's immortality: "I think that Celia Cruz will always be with us. Her personality, her music, her humanity have delved deeply into the hearts of the Latin world."[42]

CELIA CRUZ BROUGHT CUBA TO THE WORLD

Celia Cruz touched hearts not only in the Latin world but also the entire world. Her voice and her music reached all corners of the world and transcended racial, ethnic, and language barriers. She brought her music and her love of Cuba to the entire world.

CELIA CRUZ, FIDEL CASTRO, AND CUBA

Celia Cruz remained a very outspoken opponent of Fidel Castro for the remainder of her life, refusing to set foot on Cuban soil until he was overthrown. For his part, Castro refused to allow her to return to the island. Cruz went so far as to refuse to perform with any musician who did travel to Cuba, and for several years, she would not appear onstage with Oscar D'León, a Venezuelan musician who visited Havana in 1983 with his orchestra, because she viewed his trip as a betrayal.

In 1993, Cruz held a press conference in Colombia and criticized Cuba's legalization of the American dollar (formerly, possession of American currency meant 20 years in a Cuban jail). That same year, during a performance at the Summit of the Americas in Miami, Cruz implored the world leaders who were present, "In the name of my fellow Cubans, please stop aiding and abetting Fidel Castro. If you stop helping him, he'll have to give up power, and only then will Cuba be a free country. Please, help my people."[*]

Celia Cruz never realized her dream of seeing Cuba free of Castro's communist regime. She spent more than half her life dreaming of returning to a free Cuba but died in exile. The Cuban soil in her casket was the closest she was able to come to being buried in her beloved homeland.

*Celia Cruz, with Ana Christina Reymundo. *Celia: My Life*. New York: HarperCollins, 2004, p. 179.

Through her powerful voice and charismatic personality, she spread awareness of Cuban music around the world and became a major influence on Latin culture everywhere. By singing only in Spanish, she appealed to Hispanics the world over. She dominated the Latin music scene for half of the twentieth century, even into the twenty-first, spending more than 50 years as one of the most popular Cuban artists in the world.

The love she felt for her homeland was still evident in her song lyrics up until the end of her life; for example, in the 1998 song "From Havana to Here," she sang:

> From Havana to here there is a current that calls me
> With the flavor of tobacco, son-montuno, rum, and guava
> I don't want you to say anything else
> Just let me keep on dreaming
> That from Havana to here there is a current that calls me.[43]

Her manager, Omer Pardillo-Cid, who considered Cruz to be his adoptive mother, gave an apt summary of the relationship between Cruz and her native country when he spoke at her funeral: "You left Cuba, but Cuba never left you."[44] Indeed, to the nearly 2 million Cubans living outside Cuba, Celia Cruz served as a reminder of what they had left behind. Cruz once stated: "In exile, I have learned to be Cuban in a way that might not have been possible if I had stayed in Cuba. I think being an exile has taught me to love my country even more."[45]

TRIBUTES TO CELIA CRUZ

There have been numerous tributes to the Queen of Salsa since her death. On September 3, 2003, Marc Anthony, Gloria Estefan, and Olga Tañón led a tribute to Celia Cruz during the fourth annual Latin Grammy Awards. They were joined in honoring the Queen of Salsa by Arturo Sandoval, La India, Victor Manuelle, El General, and reunited members of the Fania All Stars.

CELIA CRUZ'S LEGACY

THE HUMANITARIAN WORK OF CELIA CRUZ

Celia Cruz's legacy transcends her lasting influence on music and includes humanitarian causes. In 2002, she established the Celia Cruz Foundation; her manager and "adopted" son, Omer Pardillo-Cid, serves as the president of the nonprofit organization. One mission of the foundation is to help young Hispanic musicians of limited economic means further their education by offering them scholarships in her name. Another mission is to help raise money for the battle against cancer. Because cancer had claimed the life of her mother, Cruz had been a longtime volunteer for efforts to help raise awareness and funds in this arena, and for years she had donated her time and talent to the annual marathon of the League Against Cancer in Miami. She had helped raise millions of dollars to pay for the treatment of cancer patients who otherwise would not have been able to afford medical care. The Celia Cruz Foundation Web site notes, "Throughout her career, Celia welcomed every opportunity to lend her voice in support of charities worldwide."*

In addition to her foundation, Cruz had long been involved in humanitarian causes. For example, she donated funds to help build homes for poor children in several Latin American countries, including Peru, Nicaragua, Venezuela, Honduras, and Costa Rica. Most of her efforts on behalf of these charitable and noble causes were done anonymously. Pedro Knight explained that his wife did not perform her acts of generosity to gain media attention, but rather out of the genuine goodness of her heart. He explained, "She was not like many other artists who do something and then reveal it to all the media. Celia has done hundreds of good things around the world, and she never spoke about them. . . . She has devoted her time and talent to good causes."**

---

*The Celia Cruz Foundation, "Celebrity Friends." http://www.celiacruzfoundation.org/friends. html.

**Quoted in Eduardo Marceles, *Azúcar! The Biography of Celia Cruz.* New York: Reed Press, 2004, p. 175.

Union City, New Jersey, which has one of the largest Cuban populations in the United States outside Miami, opened the Celia Cruz Park on June 3, 2004. The park has a walk of fame with 20 stars for noted entertainers. In addition, a monument in Union City was dedicated in Cruz's honor after her death.

Other tributes would follow. On August 15, 2006, the Smithsonian National Museum of American History debuted a traveling exhibit in her honor in Washington, D.C., titled *¡Azúcar! The Life and Music of Celia Cruz*. It highlighted her career through samples of her music, videos, photos, personal documents, rare footage, and costumes. The exhibition showcased her early appearances on Cuban radio, her years with the Sonora Matancera, and her later collaborations with Tito Puente, the Fania All Stars, Johnny Pacheco, Willie Colón, and others. The costumes include one she wore in the early 1950s for a performance in a Havana nightclub, as well as the gown she wore at her last public appearance shortly before her death. Also included in the exhibit are several pairs of her famous shoes with the unimaginably high, recessed heel. Also on display were Pedro Knight's trumpet and the couple's 1962 marriage license from the state of Connecticut. The national tour of the exhibit continued through 2009, with stops all over the United States, including New York City and Miami.

In addition to the traveling exhibit, a musical based on the life of Celia Cruz debuted in September 2007. With shows performed either all in Spanish or all in English, the musical, titled simply *Celia: The Life and Music of Celia Cruz*, debuted in New York. From there the show toured the United States and Latin America, keeping the memory of the Queen of Salsa alive for her many fans who attended the show. The tribute to Cruz was produced by David Maldonado and Henry Cardenas, who described it as

the story of an artist's love for her country revealed through a musical life that spans for more than 60 years. Throughout

Since Cruz's death, different people and organizations have paid tribute to her. With her work and her life honored in museum exhibits, concerts, and public memorials, Cruz's family and fans have ensured that the Queen of Salsa will continue to influence future generations.

her career, Ms. Cruz faces constant successes as well as challenges. . . .

She shares her victories and disillusions with the love of her life, Pedro Knight, and dreams of one day returning to her country. However, that dream is challenged when she is denied a visa to visit her dying mother, and then realizes that she may never again return to her beloved Cuba.[46]

Cristina Saralegui, Cuban-American journalist, actress, and talk show host, gave Cruz a fitting tribute when she called her "a source of infinite wisdom, a live example of integrity, decency, and love." Saralegui went on to say, "Celia Cruz, you are, and always will be, the color of my flag, the taste of my country, the little lighthouse that makes me able to find myself. Your voice and the sound of your laughter will live in me forever."[47]

Chronology

1925 Úrsula Hilaria Celia Caridad Cruz Alfonso is born on October 21 in Santos Suárez, a poor section of Havana, Cuba.

1938 Named Queen of the Conga at a radio talent show at Radio Lavín in Havana.

1945–1949 Attends teachers college, the Escuela Normal para Maestros, in Havana.

1947 Wins her first cake in a radio talent contest, *La Hora del Té* (Tea Time), at Radio García Serra in Havana.

1947–1950 Studies voice, music theory, and piano at the Conservatorio Nacional de Música, Havana's National Conservatory of Music.

1950 Joins the Sonora Matancera.

1925
Úrsula Hilaria Celia Caridad Cruz Alfonso is born on October 21

1947–1950
Studies voice, music theory, and piano at the Conservatorio Nacional de Música

1962
Marries Pedro Knight on July 14

1925 — 1962

1945–1949
Attends teachers college

1960
Celia Cruz and the members of the Sonora Matancera flee Cuba for Mexico

1960   Celia Cruz and the members of the Sonora Matancera flee Cuba for Mexico. Later they will settle in the United States.

1962   Celia Cruz marries Pedro Knight on July 14.

1973   Appears in the Latin musical production *Hommy* and sings on the album by the same name.

1974   *Celia y Johnny* released.

1990   Wins her first Grammy Award, for Best Tropical Latin Performance, which she shared with Ray Baretto for their album *Ritmo en el Corazón*.

1992   Appears in the Hollywood film *The Mambo Kings*.

2003   Dies in her home in Fort Lee, New Jersey.

1973
Appears in the Latin musical production *Hommy* and sings on the album by the same name

1992
Appears in the Hollywood film *The Mambo Kings*

1973

2003

1990
Wins her first Grammy Award, for Best Tropical Latin Performance, which she shared with Ray Baretto for their album *Ritmo en el Corazón*

2003
Dies in her home in Fort Lee, New Jersey

Notes

Chapter 1

1 Quoted in Eduardo Marceles, *Azúcar! The Biography of Celia Cruz*. New York: Reed Press, 2004, p. 256.

2 Quoted in Alexis Rodriguez-Duarte, *Presenting Celia Cruz*. New York: Clarkson Potter, 2004, p. 19.

3 Marceles, *Azúcar!* pp. 107–108.

4 Quoted in Rodriquez-Duarte, *Presenting Celia Cruz*, p. 42.

5 Mirta Ojito, "America's Queen of Salsa: Singer's Popularity Rides Waves of Immigration," *New York Times*, June 27, 1998. http://www.nytimes.com/1998/06/27/nyregion/america-s-queen-of-salsa-singer-s-popularity-rides-waves-of-immigration.html?scp=1&sq=Mirta%20Ojito,%20%22America's%20Queen%20of%20Salsa:%20Singer's%20Popularity%20Rides%20Waves%20of%20Immigration,%22&st=cse.

6 Quoted in Marceles, *Azúcar!* p. 41.

7 Quoted in Elizabeth Llorente, "Celia Cruz: Salsa Star, Expatriate, Whirlwind," *New York Times*, August 30, 1987. http://www.nytimes.com/1987/08/30/arts/celia-cruz-salsa-star-expatriate-whirlwind.html?scp=7&sq=celia%20cruz&st=cse&pagewanted=1.

8 Enrique Fernandez, "Talent in Action: Celia Cruz," *Billboard*, November 6, 1982, p. 40.

9 Quoted in Rodriquez-Duarte, *Presenting Celia Cruz*, p. 58.

10 Quoted in Llorente, "Celia Cruz: Salsa Star, Expatriate, Whirlwind."

11 Quoted in Marceles, *Azúcar!* p. 81.

Chapter 2

12 Celia Cruz, with Ana Christina Reymundo. *Celia: My Life*. New York: HarperCollins, 2004, p. 17.

13 Ibid., p. 22.

14 Ibid., p. 23.

Chapter 3

15 Quoted in Marceles, *Azúcar!* p. 16.

16 Ibid.

17 Cruz, with Reymundo, *Celia*, p. 34.

Chapter 4

18 Quoted in Marceles, *Azúcar!* p. 46.

19 Ibid., p. 45.

20 Cruz, with Reymundo, *Celia*, pp. 58–59.

21 Ibid., p. 66.

Chapter 5

22 Cruz, with Reymundo, *Celia*, p. 80.

23 Ibid., p. 80.

24 Cruz, with Reymundo, *Celia*, p. 82.

25 Ibid., p. 87.

26 Ibid., p. 88.

27 Quoted in Rodriquez-Duarte, *Presenting Celia Cruz*, p. 19.

Chapter 6

28 Quoted in César Miguel Rondón, *The Book of Salsa*. Chapel Hill: University of North Carolina Press, 2008, p. 132.

29 Celia Cruz and Johnny Pacheco, *Celia y Johnny*, Vaya Records, 1974.

Chapter 7

30 Quoted in Rodriguez-Duarte, *Presenting Celia Cruz*, p. 79.

31 Ibid., p. 45.

32 Quoted in Llorente, "Celia Cruz: Salsa Star, Expatriate, Whirlwind."

Chapter 8

33 Smithsonian Institution, "Celia Cruz's Shoes." History Wired. http://historywired.si.edu/object.cfm?ID=90.

34 Congressional Tribute to Celia Cruz Act. HR 149. January 4, 2005. http://thomas.loc.gov/.cgi-bin/query/z?c109:H.R.+149:

35 Quoted in Llorente, "Celia Cruz: Salsa Star, Expatriate, Whirlwind."

Chapter 9

36 Quoted in Marceles, *Azúcar!* p. 254.

37 Cruz, with Reymundo, *Celia*, p. 74.

38 Quoted in Marceles, *Azúcar!* p. 98.

39 Quoted in Rodriguez-Duarte, *Presenting Celia Cruz*, p. 90.

40 Ibid., p. 38.

41 Ibid., p. 78.

42 Ibid., p. 76.

43 Celia Cruz, *Azúcar Negra*, RMM Records, 1998.

44 Quoted in Marceles, *Azúcar!* p. 4

45 Cruz with Reymundo, *Celia*, p. 124.

46 Quoted in Latina Viva, "Musical Will Tell the Story of Celia Cruz," April 27, 2007. http://www.latinaviva.com/50226711/musical_will_tell_the_story_of_celia_cruz.php.

47 Quoted in Rodriguez-Duarte, *Presenting Celia Cruz*, p. 100.

Bibliography

Books

Cruz, Celia, with Ana Christina Reymundo. *Celia: My Life*. New York: HarperCollins, 2004.

Marceles, Eduardo. *Azúcar! The Biography of Celia Cruz*. New York: Reed Press, 2004.

Rodriguez-Duarte, Alexis. *Presenting Celia Cruz*. New York: Clarkson Potter, 2004.

Rondón, César Miguel. *The Book of Salsa*. Chapel Hill: University of North Carolina Press, 2008.

Steward, Sue. *Música! Salsa, Rumba, Merengue, and More*. San Francisco: Chronicle Books, 1999.

Periodicals

Abreu, Christina. "Celebrity, 'Crossover,' and Cubanidad: Celia Cruz as 'La Reina de Salsa,' 1971–2003." *Latin American Music Review* 28, no. 1, Spring/Summer 2007.

Cooper, Carol. "Our Lady of Perpetual Salsa." *Village Voice*, October 30, 1990.

Fernandez, Enrique. "Talent in Action: Celia Cruz." *Billboard*, November 6, 1982.

Llorente, Elizabeth. "Celia Cruz: Salsa Star, Expatriate, Whirlwind." *New York Times*, August 30, 1987. Available online. URL: http://www.nytimes.com/1987/08/30/arts/celia-cruz-salsa-star-expatriate-whirlwind.html?scp=7&sq=celia%20cruz&st=cse&pagewanted=1

Ojito, Mirta. "America's Queen of Salsa: Singer's Popularity Rides Waves of Immigration." *New York Times*, June 27, 1998. Available online. URL: http://www.nytimes.com/1998/06/27/nyregion/america-s-queen-of-salsa-singer-s-popularity-rides-waves-of-immigration.html?scp=1&sq=Mirta%20Ojito,%20%22America's%20Queen%20of%20Salsa:%20Singer's%20Popularity%20Rides%20Waves%20of%20Immigration,%22&st=cse

Wadey, Paul. "Celia Cruz: Energetic Singer Known as the 'Queen of Salsa.'" *Independent*, July 18, 2003. Available online. URL: www.independent.co.uk/news/obituaries/celia-cruz-548437.html

Watrous, Peter. "With a Voice Euphoric and Strong." *New York Times*, July 4, 1995. Available online. URL: http://www.nytimes.

com/1995/07/04/arts/jazz-festival-review-with-a-voice-euphoric-and-strong.html

Web Sites

Active Musician. "Celia Cruz Biography." Available online. URL: http://www.activemusician.com/Celia-Cruz-Biography--t8i3428

Gale—Free Resources. "Hispanic Heritage: Celia Cruz." Available online. URL: http://www.gale.cengage.com/free_resources/chh/bio/cruz_c.htm

Harris, Craig. "Artist Biography—Celia Cruz," Billboard. Available online. URL: http://www.billboard.com/bbcom/bio/index.jsp?pid=30846

Havana Journal. "Celia Cruz, Queen of Salsa, Dies after Cancer Battle," July 17, 2003. Available online. URL: http://havanajournal.com/culture/entry/celia_cruz_queen_of_salsa_dies_after_cancer_battle/

Sanabria, Izzy. "Celia Cruz: A Look at the Glorious Life and the Musical Career of the Queen of Salsa," Salsa Magazine.com. Available online. URL: http://www.salsamagazine.com/index.php?page=16

Smithsonian Institution. "Celia Cruz's Shoes." History Wired. Available online. URL: http://historywired.si.edu/object.cfm?ID=90

Smithsonian National Museum of American History. ¡Azúcar! The Life and History of Celia Cruz. Available online. URL: http://americanhistory.si.edu/celiacruz/main.asp?lang=fZc5353163882aLnQ

Further Reading

Books

Brown, Monica. *My Name Is Celia/Me Llamo Celia*. Flagstaff, Ariz.: Luna Rising, 2004.

Chambers, Veronica. *Celia Cruz, Queen of Salsa*. New York: Dial, 2005.

Da Coll, Ivar. *¡Azúcar!* New York: Lectorium, 2005.

January, Brendan. *Fidel Castro: Cuban Revolutionary*. New York: Franklin Watts, 2003.

Leymarie, Isabelle. *Cuban Fire: The Story of Salsa and Latin Jazz*. London and New York: Continuum, 2002.

Sciurba, Katie. *Oye, Celia!* New York: Henry Holt, 2007.

Films

The Eternal Voice of Celia Cruz. DVD. Xenon Pictures, 2003.

Celia the Queen. Available online. URL: http://www.celiathequeen.com

Web Sites

The Celia Cruz Foundation
http://www.celiacruzfoundation.org

Celia Cruz Official Website
http://www.celiacruz.com

Fania
http://www.fania.com

Index

Picture Credits

About the Author

Cherese Cartlidge is a freelance writer and editor. She holds a bachelor's degree in psychology from New Mexico State University and a master's degree in education from the University of Georgia. She has taught language arts, reading, social studies, and math. Her first love, however, has always been writing. She is the author of 10 nonfiction books for juveniles and young adults, ranging in topic from the Crusades to World War II and from alternative energy to reparations for slavery. Cartlidge currently lives in Georgia with her two children, who became Celia Cruz fans during the writing of this book.

112